To: Mommy

From: Courtney

Date: 11/12/98

I love you
with all my heart

THANKS, MOM, FOR EVERYTHING

Thanks, Mom, for Everything

Susan Alexander Yates
&Allison Yates Gaskins

SERVANT PUBLICATIONS
ANN ARBOR, MICHIGAN

Vine Books is an imprint of Servant Publications especially
designed to serve evangelical Christians.

All Scripture quotations, unless otherwise indicated, are taken
from the HOLY BIBLE, NEW INTERNATIONAL VERSION.
© 1973, 1978, 1984 by International Bible Society. Used by
permission of Zondervan Publishing House. All rights reserved.

Published by Servant Publications
P.O. Box 8617
Ann Arbor, Michigan 48107

Cover design: Left Coast Design, Portland, Oregon
Cover illustration: Camille Przewodek

97 98 99 00 01 10 9 8 7 6 5 4 3 2 1

Printed in the United States of America
ISBN 1-56955-017-4

LIBRARY OF CONGRESS CATALOGING-IN-PUBLICATION DATA

Yates, Susan Alexander.
Thanks, Mom, for everything / Susan Alexander Yates and Allison
Yates Gaskins.
    p.   cm.
ISBN 1-56955-017-4
1. Mothers and daughters—Literary collections.   2. Mothers—
Literary collections.   I. Gaskins, Allison Yates.   II. Title.
PN6071.M7Y38   1997
306.874'3—dc21   96-53836
                                                  CIP

Contents

Introduction

❧

There are no perfect moms, or mothers-in-law, or grannys, or.... But you know that. In fact, there are no perfect people! So this isn't a book about perfection, but about *appreciation*. Many moms feel tired, guilty, frustrated, and unappreciated. It's time to choose to appreciate the women in our lives, and so with this book we choose to honor them and to thank them.

We are especially thankful for those women in our own families who have influenced us—Frances Alexander, Sue Tucker Yates, Jan Gaskins, Susy Allison, and Grandmas Alexander, Ferguson, and Gaskins. God has used each one of them in unique ways to encourage, to exhort, and to mold us. We have found that God gives each of us exactly the family we need to help us grow into the women he has created us to be. Sometimes growth is painful and slow. Relationships may be hurtful or awkward. Yet as we trust God in each relationship, he will use them for good in our lives.

We appreciate the many men and women who have shared openly in this book about the special relationships in their lives. Some of their names have been changed to protect their privacy. But all of the stories are true.

We pray that you might be encouraged, as we have, as you get to know some amazing women in the following pages.

May each of us take the time today to say "thank you" to the special "moms" in our lives.

Teenage Misery

Trying to control the tears streaming down my face, I knocked on the door to Mom and Dad's room. My eyes were puffy from crying and my face red with anger and humiliation. Mom was already curled up in bed with a book, but when she saw my miserable state she quickly put her book down and moved over so I could curl up on the bed beside her.

"Nancy makes me so mad!" I sobbed. "She and Amy have decided to be best friends and they think they are *so* cool. They are always whispering, and I just know they are talking about me and making fun of me. They eat lunch together and make it plain that they don't want *me* to be a part of their group. And they've invited Sophie to eat with them! She was *my* friend, but now she wants to spend time with *them* instead of *me*. They've become the 'cool' group and I'm not in it. I'm all left out and I don't have any friends! They're all popular and I'm not. I'm not even smart or a great athlete. I'm not in the 'in group' and no one likes me."

I was thirteen years old, and I was miserable. Large for my age, I towered over the boys in my classes. Thick glasses helped my badly nearsighted eyes but contributed nothing to my looks. My buck

9

teeth were restrained by thick, unsightly braces. Pimples popped up in the most obvious places. I was not a beauty—at least not to anyone but my parents.

"Susan, sweetheart," my mom began when my torrent of tears and fury finally subsided and I began to relax in the security of her comforting embrace, "I think you are beautiful. I think you are smart and fun to be with. Sometimes the girls that are considered 'cool' in the junior high years aren't the most well liked in the later teen years. I am not the least bit worried. I know you are beautiful and wonderful. Be patient. Even though it doesn't seem like it right now, this awful time will pass. Your turn will come. You will have close friends. You will have a special place."

Thanks, Mom, for not panicking or overreacting to my misery. Instead you gave me the comfort of your arms and your understanding. You believed in me when I felt no one else did. You gave me the perspective I lacked, and most of all, you gave me hope.

Laura's Letter

Dear Mom,

As I sit gazing at this beautiful little boy in my arms, this precious one that I love more than almost anything, I am finally beginning to realize the depth of *your* love for me. It is hard to imagine that anyone else could love a child as much as I love Chase. Yet, I am realizing now that you have loved me with the same reckless abandon since before I was even born and you have given your life to caring for me since the day I arrived. I'm sorry it has taken so long for me to appreciate all that you have done for me!

I think of how eager I was to become pregnant and how overjoyed I was the day I found out I was going to have a baby. I was immediately enthralled with the tiny child inside of me. I understand now that you also were excited about having a baby—me. You loved me from the first day you knew of my existence. You dreamed about *me*, made happy plans for *me,* dedicated your life to loving *me*—just as I have done for Chase. It's funny to think of you and Dad picking out names for me and decorating my nursery. I am reminded of all the things that come along with pregnancy—stretch marks, nausea, a huge stomach, emotional craziness, then finally LABOR! You did it all for me—and that was just to bring me into this world. From that day on you lovingly changed thousands of stinky diapers, nursed until you were sore, were thrown up on, and went months without more than three or four hours of sleep per night! Just as much as I have loved doing all of this for my son, I know you treasured doing it for me—in spite of the wearisome tasks—simply because you loved me.

You did so much for me, Mom! You sacrificed financially to stay home and be there for me. You gave up your social life in exchange for days and nights of feeding, bathing, tutoring, encouraging, entertaining, chauffeuring, and nurturing me. I can't remember if, as a child, I expressed any gratitude to you for your love for me... but I *know* that I didn't thank you much as a teenager! You volunteered for almost every activity, sport, or club I was involved in, and I often just ignored you. You wanted to know about me—my feelings, friends, boyfriends—and I pushed you away, wondering "Why does my Mom have to be so nosy?" I definitely didn't want your advice or even give you credit for having any wisdom at all! Why is youth so blind?

What I didn't realize was that to you, I was still that precious little baby girl you had cared for and nurtured and held so close. When I hold Chase, he looks up at me so lovingly. He is always hugging me and wanting me just to sit with him and hold him. I know that right now I am the most important person in his life. I provide for all his needs. I am more necessary to him than anything or anyone else, and

I treasure that feeling of acceptance. I want to freeze these moments because I know that one day in the not so distant future he, too, will push his once-adored mom away. When I was small you were everything to me, and yet only a decade later I began trying to distance myself from you. I know that this is a natural part of growing up, but I dread the day when Chase begins to do the same. That must have been so hard for you, Mom, after you had given so much of yourself for me for so long.

Thanks for being patient with me, Mom. It took twenty-five years, but now that I too am a mother, I am catching glimpses of what your life has been like. I know some of what you have sacrificed for me. You have done so much, only to be appreciated so little. I want to begin right now to express my gratitude to you. Thank you for standing by me, in spite of the times when I didn't understand why you were around or even want you to be there. Thank you for knowing what was good for me, even when I thought I knew better. You may not have realized it at the time, but you have been a model for me. I look to your example as I now raise my own family. I hope I can be as loving and as unselfish a mother as you have been. Thank you.

Love, Laura

Thanks, Mom, for everything.

You Stood by Me

᠆᠊ᢌᢀᢘ᠊᠆

M y period was late, but I didn't think too much about it. I just knew I couldn't be pregnant. *Surely* that couldn't happen to *me*.

Mom knew about the relationship I had with my boyfriend. It was clear that she disapproved. We'd had many talks about sex, and I knew that she believed God's plan for sexual intimacy was that it be saved exclusively for marriage. But I just couldn't see the reasoning behind her thinking—or at least I didn't want to. I knew Mom was worried about me, and that both bothered and annoyed me because we were close.

Finally she said to me, "Stacy, do you think you could be pregnant? I think you should take a pregnancy test."

Her comment really shook me because I was beginning to wonder myself. Summoning up courage, I decided to follow her advice.

It was a busy weekend for our family. Mom and Dad had taken our out-of-town company sightseeing, and I was finally alone and able to do the test. I was anxious as I waited for the results. When I saw the clear positive sign I almost threw up. Nervous, badly frightened, and in tears, I curled up on the couch and waited for Mom to come home. I felt so ashamed. I knew how devastated my parents were going to be. Even though I was twenty years old and could legally have an abortion, I knew I could never do that. I valued life too much. I was in agony. What would I do? What would Mom say?

Mom's response was amazing. She held me in her arms and let me cry. Her response was, "Stacy, we will get through this."

She could have said, "I told you so." She could have gone on about how I'd let her and Dad down, how I had disobeyed God, how I had messed up my life. But she didn't.

Instead we began a difficult journey—but we began it *together*. Mom and Dad didn't pressure me into any decision. They listened, they prayed for me, and they guided me to resources to help me. We all knew that *I* had to make the difficult decisions about the pregnancy and this child. With their full support I went to Liberty Home for Unwed Mothers in Lynchburg, Virginia.

Mom wrote almost every day. She called. She visited me at every opportunity. And she prayed. When I made the decision to give the baby up for adoption, she supported me.

When the time came for me to deliver, Mom was there. She stayed with me throughout a long, difficult labor and delivery. It was hard for me, but it was even harder for Mom because the day I went into labor, her own mother became ill and died. Yet she chose to stay with me because she felt I needed her the most.

Having decided that it was best to give up my baby, I knew I couldn't even hold her when she was born or I might change my mind. So it was Mom who stood in for me and into whose arms the doctor placed my baby girl.

The day of my daughter's birth was a day of double loss for Mom—the day she had to give up her first and only grandchild and the day she lost her mother. But it was a day I knew, as never before, that she loved me. She stood by me, she forgave me, and she loved me unconditionally. Because of her example, I am able to accept God's forgiveness and to believe in his unconditional love for me.

Thank you, Mom, for standing by me through one of the most painful times in your life and mine. Thank you for demonstrating to me the power of God's forgiveness and love.

Grandma, Baseball, and a Chest of Drawers

༄༅༅

Outside the bright sun was beckoning, but eight-year-old Michael was sitting miserably in a damp garage. Groaning, he looked irritably at the chest of drawers that needed to be sanded. All he really wanted to do was to run outside and play! Michael had been asked to sand the chest because Dad wanted to refinish it and put it in Grandma's bedroom. Grandma came often to visit, and this was to be Michael's contribution to making her feel at home. Grimly, Michael grasped a wad of sandpaper in his grubby fingers and set to work, giving little thought to anything but speed.

"Who cares if this thing is sanded perfectly anyway?" he muttered to himself. "If I can just rub it down enough so Dad can tell I worked at it, that will be fine and I can get outside to meet the guys!"

He rubbed indiscriminately, back and forth, up and down, grazing over the corners of the familiar old piece. His thoughts drifted out to the baseball diamond, and he mentally plotted his pitching strategy for the game he would soon be playing. The sun climbed higher outdoors, and Michael gazed longingly at the rays of sunlight which beamed across the garage floor.

"It's almost noon and I'm going to miss the ball game if I don't finish soon!" He stepped back and looked at his work with the confidence of an eight-year-old in a hurry to get somewhere.

"That looks pretty good to me!" he said aloud. But sandpaper marks were everywhere, and the uneven surface would never hold a coat of fresh paint. Such details, though, stood in the way of freedom, and what was *really* important? Getting outside to meet the guys, of course!

Michael brushed his hands on the seat of his pants with satisfaction and was just settling his cap on his head when a shadow crossed the patch of sunlight by the garage door. Grandma had come to inspect his work.

"Hey Gram!" he said jauntily as he headed outside, but her quiet "Hello" stopped him in his tracks.

"Michael," she said, gazing back and forth between her grandson and the forlorn chest of drawers. "Michael, I want to tell you something. Whatever job you are given, you should always do it the best that you can, because that job will become a part of who you are as a person." With that, she turned and quietly headed back into the house. Michael turned too and looked critically at his neglected project. It really didn't look *that* bad. There were some rough edges, to be sure, but couldn't they be covered by paint? "Do the best you can, Michael" rang in his ears. Reluctantly, he tossed his baseball cap aside and set back to work with a sigh. The game would have to wait. He had a job to finish.

Thanks, Grandma, for teaching me about the value of my work. Thank you for believing that what I do has significance and for communicating this to me with your gentle challenge to always do my best.

Mom's Sixth Sense

❧❦❧

I must have been about five or six when it happened. It was so long ago you'd think I would have forgotten, but the memory of those awful feelings of guilt, shame, and embarrassment are still vivid today.

Mom had taken me with her to a large stationery store where she had some shopping to do. I was free to wander up and down the aisles filled with attractive, enticing items. More cards, pencils, pens, and notebooks than I'd ever seen! At my age, though, I was mesmerized by the huge bunches of brightly colored rubber bands. So many colors, so many bands! What fun it would be to have those, to be able to shoot them, to tie them together, to show them off to my brothers.

There are so many! I'm sure it would be OK if I took just one bunch. Nobody would even notice or care, I told myself.

Glancing over my shoulder to make sure nobody was looking, I slipped a bunch of the brightly colored bands into the pocket of my jacket. Meeting my mother at the checkout counter, I tried hard to pretend that nothing was unusual.

We left the store, and I'm sure that my five-year-old attempts to cover up only made me act a bit weird, arousing an observant mother's curiosity. It seems to me that mothers have eyes in the back of their heads, some kind of a sixth sense or unusual intuitive knowledge that things aren't as they should be. Most moms don't miss much. Mine surely didn't! Watching my awkward posture as I tried to cover my bulging pocket, my mother asked,

"Susan, what are you doing? Is there something in your pocket?"

"No, Mommy," I replied.

Not to be fooled, my mother persisted, "I think there is something in your pocket. I want you to show me what it is."

Knowing I'd been found out, I carefully pulled the rubber bands out of my pocket and handed them to her. Her sad, angry look made me want to run away. But the worst was yet to come.

"Susan," she said, not mincing any words, "you took these without paying for them. That's stealing. You know that is wrong. We are going back to the store, and you will have to tell the manager what you have done and that you are sorry."

"I can't!" I wailed in utter embarrassment. "You take them in for me. I can't do that!"

"No," my wise mother replied. "*You* must do this. I will go with you, but you have to do it yourself."

Mom marched me back to the store and straight up to the manager's office where I had to confess and apologize. The manager was understanding, but stern, as he looked me in the eye and said, "I hope you never steal anything again. I hope you have learned a lesson from this!"

A lesson at that moment was the furthest thing from my mind. I knew only that I was humiliated, furious with my mother, and that I wanted to run away. The ride home was deadly silent.

It did not occur to me at that time that my mother was probably embarrassed, too. She must have been humiliated by having to tell the manager that *her* child had stolen. I'm sure the last thing she wanted to do was to go all the way back to the store and deal with this. She had other things she needed to do. She could have dismissed it by just telling me that I had been wrong and that I shouldn't do such a thing again. She could have ignored her instincts and not dealt with the issue. She could have excused it saying, "It's just a pack of rubber bands. I'll pay for them the next time I go in."

But she didn't. She was willing to be inconvenienced, to be embarrassed, and to deal with her strong-willed child who pitched a fit. Mom knew the importance of honesty. And she knew that teaching it must begin when we are young.

✿

Thanks, Mom, for noticing my actions, for catching me in my sin, and for making me learn that I have to put things right. Actions do have consequences! Thank you for seeing the big picture, for being a woman of integrity, and for teaching me that such integrity is priceless.

22

A Hunger to Grow

A white strand of hair slipped out of her bun as she leaned over to show me something she'd underlined in her Bible.

"Just look at this, Susan," Grandmother Yates said. "I read it this morning. Isn't it grand for an old lady like me?"

Taking the book from my mother-in-law, who is "Grandmother" to everyone, I read the marked passage. "They will still bear fruit in old age;/ They will stay fresh and green,/ Proclaiming, 'The Lord is upright; he is my rock and there is no wickedness in him'" (Ps 92:14-15).

How typical, I mused. *Here's this eighty-nine-year-old woman who's read the Bible for years, and she's still finding something new that speaks to her and excites her! She's still learning. She's still growing and her enthusiasm is contagious.*

A hunger to grow and a genuine interest in people have always characterized Grandmother's life. A few years ago when she decided to move from her home to a retirement community in a new town, she prayed, "Oh Lord, show me what you have to teach me in my new place. Show me what you have for me to do."

Not long after she settled in to her new home, a

great-niece came to visit her and said, "Grandmother, I'd like to give a tea, and I was wondering if you would come and share with me and some of my friends what the Bible says about angels."

Surprised, but enthusiastic, Grandmother responded, "If you are sure you want to hear from an old lady like me, I'd be delighted!"

What began three years ago as a simple Christmas tea turned into a weekly Bible study for twelve young mothers with Grandmother as their teacher. Every Monday you'll find these women sitting on the floor of Grandmother's living room asking questions about Jesus, seeking advice about raising their children, and listening to stories of God's faithfulness. God had shown Grandmother his new mission for her.

Everyone is amazed at Grandmother's vitality. Her interest in others has always made her lively and fun to be with. Her fifteen grandchildren adore her. She stays up late with them when they visit, she phones them at school, and she is eager to know all about their lives.

"Tell me about that boy you are dating," she asks. "What exactly do you like about him? Are you in love? Does he love Jesus?"

Daily she prays for each one of her children and grandchildren by name, interceding for their individual needs. When Grandmother comes to visit she wants to know, "What good books have you read lately? Have you got any good tapes to listen to?"

She loves to learn about whatever we are interested in. She makes us feel important by her desire to learn more about each of us, and she challenges us by her relentless pursuit of new ideas.

Grandmother would be the first to tell you that she isn't perfect, but she knows our heavenly Father is a forgiving Father and that he cares deeply about each of his children. When I grow older, I want to be just like Grandmother, my mother-in-law, my friend.

Thank you, Grandmother, for loving me. Thank you for asking me about my life and praying for me. Your life demonstrates that a hunger to grow and an interest in people keep us focused on God and others, instead of on ourselves. Thank you for showing me how to grow old with grace and humor.

A
Mom-Away-from-Home

As a college freshman far from home, at times I was very lonely for family life. It was wonderful to be away at school, surrounded by people my own age, but often my heart ached for the laughter of small children and the warmth of home. The church I attended had what they called an "adopt-a-student" program where families could adopt college students to give them a home-away-from-home. I didn't expect much from this program, but I signed up on a whim. It was worth a try!

Not many days later, a woman called me and introduced herself as Linda. She and her husband, Kenny, along with their two children, had been paired with me through the adopt-a-student program. She invited me to dinner the following week and apologized in advance for her messy home and the chaos I was sure to find there! I missed the happy confusion of my own family and I assured her that I certainly did not mind! When she and the children arrived in their minivan at my college dorm the following week, I climbed in and settled myself. Broken toys and stale Cheerios littered the floor. I felt immediately at ease.

This marked the beginning of a new kind of friendship for me. Linda became my mom-away-from-home. She didn't mother me in the traditional ways. She didn't remind me when to come in at night or that I should really pay more attention to my Economics homework. Instead, she gave me *herself* and welcomed me into her family. Linda provided all the things I missed most being away from home. She had me come over and we did laundry together. She called just to see how I was doing. She invited me to dinner with her family; it was nothing out of the ordinary, simply a meal served with love and a mother's touch. She even invited me to make cookies with her kids.

During exams at the end of the semester, just before the Christmas holiday, I was feeling particularly sad. It was crunch time at school, and I was studying frantically; but what I really wanted to do was get into the Christmas spirit. I missed Christmas decorations and I longed for the smells and sounds of holiday cooking and Christmas carols. Somehow, Linda knew I was feeling this way without being told. One particularly gloomy afternoon she called me and said, "Allison, the kids and I are coming by to bring you something."

Soon they arrived at the dorm. When I unwrapped the package that the children excitedly presented me, a wave of joy and gratitude washed over me. It was a tiny Christmas tree, lovingly decorated with ribbons and wooden ornaments! Linda had known exactly what I was missing most at that time—family and a sense of holiday cheer. My mom-away-from-home knew just how to encourage me!

Years later, Linda is still my mom-away-from-home. Although we no longer live in the same town, we keep in touch, and her wonderful letters encourage me greatly. I still appreciate the way she bridged the gap for me when I was no longer under my own mother's roof but still needed a gentle maternal influence. She eased my transition out of the nest by being there for me when I needed mothering!

Thank you, Linda, for being my mom-away-from-home! Thank you for welcoming me into your home and taking the time to make me feel like one of the family. You gave me comfort and a mother's love when I needed it so much!

Seeing Beauty

B ecause I was sick as a young child I wasn't able to attend school until the second grade. My mysterious fever just wouldn't go away. For a long time the doctors thought it was rheumatic fever, but a final diagnosis was never made. Days dragged by. There were good days when the fever left and my parents breathed a sigh of relief, but then it would return with a vengeance. They must have been on an emotional roller coaster, dealing with this unknown, unpredictable illness. I'm sure it was equally frustrating having to care for and entertain a sick child over such a long period of time. And yet my mother never communicated to me that it was difficult for her. Instead, she used this time as a special opportunity for positive enrichment.

When I was confined to bed, Mom brought my meals on a tray. But it wasn't just any old tray. It was a tray designed for a princess. On it Mom placed the best china, a folded linen napkin, and in a vase a lovely flower in colors coordinated to the napkin Mom had chosen. Her attention to detail and beauty made me feel that I was worth fussing over, that I was important.

And then there were the "button-jewels." Mom brought me jars of gorgeous, unusual buttons of different vintages and sizes. In time my bedroom became a fancy jewelry shop—a boutique of precious stones, with display trays of vast treasures Mom had brought me. If I tired of my "jewels" Mom brought out her collection of old wallpaper and we made paper doll dresses. Even paper with an ugly, old flamingo pattern was transformed into a designer paper doll's gown—worthy of Miss America.

During that time of illness I learned to sew and to appreciate beautiful embroidery. "Elaine," Mom would say as she showed me a delicate piece of hardanger stitchery, "just imagine all the work that went into this beautiful piece. Isn't it gorgeous? You could do something like this!"

During those years Mom instilled in me a love for reading. Each morning after breakfast, we read from Catherine F. Vos' *The Child's Story Bible*. And in the night when I would awaken unable to breathe, Mom would hold me on her lap while the shower ran full steam for vapor, and she would read. Listening to the stories eased my panic and helped me settle down and breathe more easily.

We read through the classics. *Little Women, Black Beauty*, and *The Five Little Peppers* became my dear friends.

Mom always looked for beauty in unexpected places. Whether it was a place setting on a tray, a button collection, a blanket tenderly stitched, or the lovely words of literature, she always pointed out the beauty to me and, in so doing, taught *me* to look for beauty in every situation. Her creativity encouraged me to be creative. As an adult I still find that in times of stress, I am refreshed as I turn to sewing or to creating a lovely meal or flower arrangement. Creating and looking for beauty help me regain a positive perspective in this often negative world.

Thanks, Mom, for showing this sick little girl that she wasn't a bother. Thank you for using those difficult years to show me how to look for beauty and how to be creative. You turned my sickbed into a creative learning center!

Honor Your Father

L eslie and David's parents were separated when Leslie was five and David was one year old. The ensuing divorce was an unhappy one, as divorces usually are, and the children were caught between both parents in bitter court cases for many years.

Beth is a woman of strength and determination. "She nearly wore herself out being my mom," explains Leslie. A newly-single mother raising two children in Washington, D.C., faces many challenges. But Beth did her best to teach her children to respect and love their father, even though their situation would naturally have led them to feel otherwise. And David and Leslie agree that one of the most important things their mother did for them was to teach them to love their father, even though she herself no longer did. Beth encouraged them to send their father birthday cards and Father's Day cards and to go willingly to visit him and his new wife in their home. She taught her children the importance of keeping their father abreast of the everyday events of their lives. Repeatedly, Beth encouraged her children to call their father to see how he was doing, just for the sake of keeping their relationship going. She never related to Leslie and David the hurt she felt as a result of her breakup with their father, but instead focused on teaching them to care for him.

Even beyond these everyday situations, Beth was forced to make personal sacrifices to help her children see that their relationship with their father was important. Perhaps the most unusual sacrifice came when the children's father moved to Morocco and demanded that Leslie and David come to visit them there. Naturally, a parent would not want to send two young children (then ages eight and four) on such a long overseas flight by themselves. Beth, having no other options, agreed to escort them herself. To do so, she had to take three weeks off from her job, travel halfway around the world, and spend two weeks in a frighteningly foreign city where the only person she knew was her estranged husband.

Looking back on that trip, Leslie acknowledges, "That must have been the worst time of Mom's life. I'm sure she hated every minute of the trip. We had to stay in hotel rooms because Dad was not yet moved into his home. Mom and I stayed in one room, and Dad and David slept in the next... sort of. Actually, every night David would come crying into our room and sleep with us. I didn't realize then, but I do now, how horrible that whole experience must have been for Mom. Even while we were there, Dad didn't take time off from work to be with us, so Mom had to take care of us all day long. Sometimes

Dad's secretary escorted us around the city, but mostly everything was left to our mom."

At that point in her life, Beth had no desire to be in Morocco, did not want to be near her former husband, and did not completely trust him with their children. Yet these things were secondary to her understanding of what was important for David and Leslie. She wanted them to grow up knowing and loving their father, because he *was* their father, and she was willing to make any sacrifice necessary to that end. In many ways, through deceit, unfairness, and endless court cases, Leslie and David's father made life difficult for their mother. Even so, Beth did not teach her children hate and despair, although she certainly felt those emotions at times. After a few years their father moved closer to their home. From that point on, visits with him were less complicated than a trip around the world and not quite as hard on Beth. David and Leslie are now adults and can recognize flaws in their father's behavior. In spite of this, and thanks to their mother's determination, they have learned to love and respect him simply because he is their father.

✿

*Thanks, Mom, for teaching us to love
our father. Thank you for not cursing
him and telling us bad things about
him, when you so easily could have.
We know he made your life very
painful. Thank you for sacrificing
your own pride and comfort to help us
spend time with him and for encouraging us by your actions always to
treat him with respect.*

✿

Confide in Me

~✥~

"John," I recently asked my husband, "what do you most appreciate about your mother?" She is approaching ninety years of age. This is the story he told me.

Ever since I can remember, Mom has had the ability to talk with me as her equal although I was always fully aware that she was the adult and I was the child. She seemed to have an unusual way of confiding in me honestly about all sorts of situations, without laying a heavy burden on me. It made me feel wonderfully special and trusted. It made me feel worthy of her confidence. It made me love her and want to live up to her belief in me.

Once, when I was nine, Mom and I were in the car on the way to a Boy Scout meeting. We had had a run-in over some matter and she was feeling badly about it. Somewhere between the drugstore and the old factory on the edge of town, Mom began to tell me how sorry she was about our argument because she realized that she had spoken hastily and had been in the wrong. She apologized to me and asked me if I would forgive her. At my age I really hadn't given too much thought to the idea that adults could be wrong and could make mistakes. That day she helped me see that adults are human and fallible just like little kids, and it meant a lot to me that she wanted things to be right between the two of us.

On another occasion, it was I who was in the wrong, and Mom didn't hesitate to talk to me about that either! I had been playing at Ben's house while Mom visited with his mother. Ben had some "rough edges," and when I spent time with him it was all too easy to pick up his bad habits. Throughout the afternoon, I gave Mom some nasty looks, was disobedient, and sassed her without much concern. We left Ben's house rather quickly, and on the way home Mom said, "After an afternoon with Ben, you suddenly began to act just like him. You were whining, ignoring me when I called, and being rude and disrespectful. That is not like you at all. That's not the way we act in our family. You said things to me that you should not have. You embarrassed me and made me very ashamed of you. If you had a little child who misbehaved so badly, what do you think you would do?"

Mom says that I stammered back, "I guess I would have to give that little child a spanking." And that is exactly what she did. But in remembering that event, some forty years later, I don't remember the spanking as much as I remember Mom's sadness about my misbehavior. She told me exactly what she was thinking, why she thought I acted the way I did, and shared with me her dilemma over how to handle me. Somehow she enabled me to see the whole thing from her perspective, *as well as* from my perspective. Mom helped me to understand exactly why she had to be sure I learned a lesson from my folly.

There were other conversations with Mom which struck me as unusually open and confiding, like the time she explained that some people have problems with alcohol and that the real reason our neighbor, Mr. Smith, was behaving strangely was because he drank too much. It was important that I understood the reasons behind his abnormal behavior because he was no longer the kind and responsible person I had always known him to be. This helped me understand what was really happening.

Mom always "told it like it was" when she talked to me. Sometimes it was in great sorrow and sometimes in the heat of anger. Occasionally it was with detached coolness and often with animated excitement. Many times it was with tender compassion. Always I felt like I was getting the real scoop from my mother. I never had to guess what she thought. There was nothing hidden to fear or to wonder about. She cared enough to tell me things the way they really were.

Thank you, Mom, for being such a clear communicator and for sharing openly and honestly with me. You made me feel special and gave me confidence that you respected me, even as a little child.

Edith's Perspective

eavy dark circles hung below my eyes. My shoulders slumped with fatigue. It had been yet another night of getting up with one or another of the children about every two hours. With five children ages seven and under, including a set of twins, I was totally wiped out much of the time.

I don't think I can make it another day without sleep! I said to myself. *I think I could go days without food, but not without sleep!*

Not only was I physically exhausted, but I wasn't patient like I knew I should be. I wasn't fun like those "other mothers" I read about in the books that tell how to do it right, how to do it all, how to be true, gentle, patient, kind—a "Proverbs 31 woman." Hah! I could barely get through the days, let alone be all those things! Instead, I just felt like a miserable failure.

Grabbing my jacket, I called to my husband that I was leaving for a few minutes—it was *his* turn to be in charge! I ran out the door, hurried across the grass to my neighbor's house, and knocked on her door. Relief surged through my whole being when Edith answered the door and warmly welcomed me in just as I burst into tears.

"Oh, Edith, I'm such a terrible mother! I'm so tired and some days I don't even like my children. I don't seem to be doing anything right. I *know* I'm a drain on my husband. I feel stuck in a rut with no end in sight."

With compassion born of years of experience, Edith listened as I poured out my frustrations to her. Her wrinkled eighty-year-old hands gently patted mine. Finally when my rambling ceased, she turned to me and said, "Oh, Susan dear, you are not a bad mother. You are a very good mother. What you are feeling is normal. It's this season in your life. It will pass. You are doing just fine."

A calm sense of "it's all-right-ness" slowly worked its way into my soul, and by the time I left Edith's house I was feeling better. Still tired, yes. Still a bit overwhelmed... but at peace.

That wasn't the only time I ran to Edith in tears. There would be many more times ahead. But each time I escaped to her shelter, I came away with a renewed sense of "all-right-ness."

Edith gave me several wonderful gifts. She listened to me. She made time for me and didn't hurry me along. Instead, she let me pour out my heart to her. But she also gave me another gift—perspective. As a mother, grandmother, and great-grandmother, she had been where I was in my life. She understood how I was feeling. My feelings didn't seem silly or stupid to her. She knew what I was going through, and she didn't panic. She had the wisdom to know that I would be fine. Edith's perspective gave me confidence.

Thank you, Edith, for taking time to listen to me, for giving me the freedom to cry and to be honest about how I felt. Thank you for giving me perspective when I didn't have any. Thank you for being there.

Let's Sing a Thankful Song

*O*n a gently sloping hillside in North Carolina, a mother and her three-year-old daughter are slowly rocking back and forth in a hammock, enjoying the breeze of the early morning....

"Gracie?"

"Yes, Mommy?"

"Let's sing a song."

"Okay! I like songs!"

"Let's sing a thankful song, Gracie."

"Was' 'dat?"

"It's a song where we tell God things we are thankful for."

"Oh. How do we do 'dat?"

"I'll show you. Just listen." The mother sang:

Thank you, Lord, for this fine day!
Thank you, Lord, for this fine day!
Thank you, Lord, for this fine day,
Right where we are!"

"T'ank you Lord, Mommy?"

"That's right! We think of things we are thankful for and sing it to God. He loves to hear people sing, especially little girls!"

"Okay, Mommy! Let's sing!"

"What are we going to thank God for?"

"Ummmm...butterflies!"

"Good idea, Gracie! Here, let's take turns choosing something to thank God for. You sing one thanks, Gracie, and I'll sing the next." And so they sang:

Thank you, Lord, for butterflies,
Thank you Lord for mommies and daddies,
Thank you Lord for hammocks that swing,
Thank you Lord for Grandma MomMom,
Thank you Lord for baby brothers,
Thank you Lord...

Thank you, Mom, for giving me the gift of a thankful heart. Thank you for modeling this to me in simple ways when I was very young, and for keeping a spirit of gratitude through the years.

One Woman to Another

The late Eugenia Price has become my favorite author. Perhaps this is because her books center around family relationships, and I identify with them so well. In her novel, *Where Shadows Go*, one of her characters expresses my thoughts exactly. She says, "There comes a time, or I've always believed there should come a time, when a mother and daughter mature into being real friends... one woman to another." I have been truly blessed with a mother who has also become my friend. I cannot put a finger on a particular time or place when this happened. In fact, I believe it was a growing process rather than an overnight transformation in our relationship. I don't believe there is a specific formula for initiating this change, though I do recall many things my mother has said or done which have given me the assurance that she considers me her friend and confidante, instead of simply her daughter.

When I married, like Mom, I suddenly became a wife with a husband and in-laws, and I was faced with a rapidly changing identity. We laughed one day recently when we realized we had both spent the day shopping with our respective mothers-in-law. What fun to share such simple events and to have a new level of "connectedness"!

But our evolution to friendship began long before this. Mom laid the foundation all through my childhood, when she was unafraid to act like a child with us and to have sheer *fun* with her children. She was even better at crawling through the mud than I was, and she always had such ingenious ideas for creating excitement! As I grew and changed, she shared in new ways with me and showed me another side of herself. She shared her weaknesses, and she also taught me some of the struggles I would face as a woman.

The conversation we shared just a few nights before I went to college was evidence of our new relationship. I had recently begun to date, and Mom wanted to prepare me for things I would face along this often treacherous road. That night she said, "Allison, you are a woman of incredible passion. Inside of you are needs and desires that you have not yet experienced in their fullness. Recognize this *now* and know that one day they will come to the surface and take you by surprise. Such passion is a good thing, but it can be overwhelming. It is important that you know *now* what depth of feeling is inside of you, that you nurture and allow this to grow carefully, but that you learn to restrain it as well. There will be a time to release this passion, but guard your heart carefully and wait for that time."

This wisdom was engraved on my heart by the sincerity with which it was spoken. I did not at that time fully understand what Mom was saying, but I trusted that one day I would. Gradually, as I began to fall in love with the man who would later become my husband, I saw the truth in the words my mother had spoken. They became her benediction on my voyage into womanhood and opened new doors of understanding and friendship.

Thanks, Mom, for allowing me to become your friend. I appreciate the risks you took in making yourself vulnerable to me. I am honored that you feel you can treat me as your equal, and I anticipate with great joy the deepening of our friendship in the years to come.

The Joy of the Lord

.⋅⋅⋅.

Twas the week before Christmas and all through the house… chaos reigned! Three small children hyper with excitement were wearing out their already exhausted parents. The children's dad was in pain from stomach ulcers. Their grandmother, who lived with them, was suffering with cataracts, and the children's mother, Susy, had recently broken her leg riding horseback. Life, it seemed, was out of control. Refusing to give in to the overwhelming temptation of despair, Susy gathered her children around her and said, "Children, what we really need to do is pray. God loves each one of us and cares about all our problems. He wants us to give them to him."

"OK, Mommy," Fitz, the youngest responded. "Can I go first?"

With a nod from Mother, the family all got down on their knees, and Fitz began, "Dear Jesus, please bless Grandmother's eyes, and Daddy's tummy, and Mommy's broke leg…."

With that, Fitz's mother dissolved into laughter. Recovering just a little, she exclaimed, "I just can't help but have a picture of these body parts—of eyes and a stomach and a leg floating up to heaven for God to bless. It is so funny!" And with that vision in mind the rest of the family began to roar with laughter, and lightheartedness replaced the sense of gloom.

Susy wasn't being disrespectful. She simply had an unusual appreciation of God's sense of humor. Her whole life reflected the joy she knew God had in his children. She also expressed this joy in her love of music. Raising her family in the South in the early part of the twentieth century, Susy was fortunate to have a wonderful old cook, Abbie, who came occasionally to help out. When Abbie was in the house it was not unusual for the kitchen to become something of a black gospel church, with Abbie teaching the fine art of "patting," clapping, singing, and dancing to gospel hymns all at the same time. Shouts of praise, squeals of laughter, and tears of joy mingled with the smell of good-old southern fried chicken.

Music and laughter were a vital part of Susy's life, but the true source of her joy was her love of the Scriptures. Her favorite verse was, "For God has not given us a spirit of fear, but of love and of joy and of sound mind" (2 Tm 1:7 KJV). Susy's Bible was well-worn and underlined. She began each morning with a Bible reading and closed each evening in the same way. It wasn't unusual for her to quote long passages of Scripture from memory. Her prayer life was a natural blend of reciting many of the promises in Scripture with her prayers for her family.

In her last days, Susy was bedridden after a partial

stroke. Yet as she lay on the hospital bed, she began to sing and to pray for each of her twelve grandchildren, their spouses, and children. As she prayed she began to recite from memory John 14. She remembered Jesus' words: "Do not let your hearts be troubled. Trust in God; trust also in me. In my Father's house are many rooms...." Her voice warmed with joy as she talked about the mansion that God was preparing for her. Tears filled the eyes of those of us who stood around her bed. We cried tears of thanksgiving for her life, her laughter, and her music, all of which were born of and fueled by the knowledge that the joy of the Lord is our strength.

Thanks, Susy FitzSimons, for the legacy you lived. Thank you for living and communicating to me, your first grandchild, and to countless others that the joy of the Lord will be our strength. You showed us all that a relationship with the Lord is to be enjoyed.

Exuberant Praise

ur humorous weekly battle began as Mom slowly backed the van out of the driveway, patiently ignoring the fact that she was the central figure in this Sunday morning ritual.

"It's not my turn!" John was quick to declare. "I sat next to her in church last week."

"And I sat next to her on Easter the week before, and you *know* that was the worst of all. I should get major bonus points for that one!" I protested vehemently.

"But it can't be my turn yet," Chris whined. "It seems like I just had to do it last week. You guys are just trying to push it off on me again."

Mom hummed a joyful little tune to herself as the battle raged on in the back seat. As our voices grew louder, so did her humming. It was a hymn of some kind, but to our stubborn, youthful ears it was just plain old noise. As far as we were concerned, Mom was warming up for an embarrassing morning of singing.

It was bad enough to have to sit next to your mother in church, but when she loved to praise the Lord as *loudly* as ours did, it was even worse! The ultimate embarrassment was the fact that she couldn't carry a tune in a bucket, let alone harmonize with the choir as she so often tried to do! Our Sunday morning challenge was to win the seat farthest away from Mom. No one wanted to have to suffer through singing alongside her. It made our ears burn, just thinking about the humiliation. And to make matters worse, Mom didn't seem to care at all how we felt. Her response to our oft-voiced complaints was "I'm not singing to you! I'm singing to the Lord, and he doesn't care what I sound like or what *you* think of it. To him, I'm making beautiful music! When I get to heaven, I'm going to be a soprano in the heavenly choir!" We just rolled our eyes and groaned when she said this. If she was going to sing with the angels, I didn't think I would be going to any of their concerts! I had to give her a little credit though; she did have more enthusiasm for praising God than just about anybody I knew.

As we settled once again into our pew at church, I breathed a sigh of relief at having won the back-seat battle. John, sitting between Mom and me, began to tense up as the organist introduced the first bars of the opening hymn. It was one of Mom's favorites, "Lift High the Cross," and as I glanced at her out of the corner of my eye, I could tell by the glow on her face that she was already transported somewhere beyond that sanctuary. Maybe she actually thought she was already in the angel choir. Before we even finished the first verse of the song she was piping away at full volume, ringing out loud and clear despite our best efforts to drown her out so that she wouldn't draw any extra attention to us. Could it be possible that she was singing even more loudly now? As we hit the refrain "I will RAISE HIM UP!" she began to lift her arms from her side and hold them up toward the heavens. I felt great pity for John who was trying desperately to pretend she wasn't really doing *that*. "Oh, God," I prayed. "Can you really enjoy this? Don't you see we're *suffering* here?!"

But then something ironic happened as I grew older. The perfect pitch I was so confident of in my childhood began to fade, and I found myself sounding more and more like my mother when I tried to sing. Could this be possible? *Please God, no!* Mom, however, never changed. She had mastered the art of ignoring her children's embarrassment and seemed to become more and more exuberant in singing her praises to the Lord. I secretly became less hesitant to sit beside her because the enthusiastic volume of her terrible voice hid my off-pitch tune! I could still sing and nobody would notice that I was straying off key as well. How had Mom learned not to care how she sounded? Was it true that to God she sounded good? Did I?

Thanks to Mom, I gradually learned the art of acceptance of my own voice and was able to praise God in spite of myself. Someday, Mom and I will *both* be sopranos in the heavenly choir!

53

Thanks, Mom, for your unabashed delight in praising your Savior. Thank you for happily ignoring our complaints and for teaching me that praise doesn't have to be perfect, it just has to be genuine! I look forward to singing with you for eternity!

What Would
Mother Do?

❧

*S*usan, how would your mother have handled this? I asked myself. My two moody teenage girls were casting gloom over our family vacation.

Should I confront them or ignore them? I wondered. Pondering what to do, I thought about my own mother. In a case like this, she would probably say, "Just ignore them and see how things are tomorrow. Part of a teenager's job is to be moody. It will pass; and if it doesn't, you can handle it later, but give it a chance to pass first."

This wasn't the first time I'd thought about how Mother might handle a situation. With five children of my own I'd thought about her numerous times as I struggled to raise them. Mother's unusual wisdom always gave me insight into my situation.

Once when our family was attending a conference, I was waiting for my mother in the lobby when I ran into an old friend. We were chatting and catching up on old times when I saw Mother heading our way. My friend turned to take her leave, but before she could I remarked, "Hey, I want you to wait and meet my mother. She's the wisest woman I've ever known."

I didn't realize the impact of what I had said until my friend replied in a thoughtful voice, "Wow! It must be amazing to be able to say that about your own mother."

Later, I thought about that surprised comment, and I began to realize in a new way how very lucky I was to have had a wise mother. It had never occurred to me that Mother was anything special when I was growing up. Instead, at times I was sure she was the meanest mom in town. We weren't allowed to watch TV on school nights. And even if we didn't have homework we were supposed to read a book. Ugh! We had chores to do daily. We were expected to have good manners, to speak to adults politely, and never to talk back to grown-ups. As teens, we had curfews, and our parents always had to know where we were and with whom. There were places we weren't allowed to go and other places we *had* to go—like church every Sunday. Life wasn't *all* rules, but as a kid I thought the balance leaned heavily in that direction. We had fun as a family. Vacations, picnics, walks and talks, and lots of hugs and "I love you's," but I didn't appreciate it then.

Even when I began to have children of my own, I didn't think about Mother's wisdom all that much. I was preoccupied with simply trying to get through each day! But as my kids grew and new challenges surfaced, I thought more and more about my mother. I began to appreciate her in new ways.

Not only has Mother's wisdom guided me in

raising my kids, it has helped my friends and those who have read the books I have authored as well. An educator by profession, Mother has an uncanny ability to recognize learning patterns in children and to provide wise counsel to parents struggling with educational options.

Where did my mother get such wisdom? She would be quick to tell you that she doesn't have any, but I know differently! Mother's wisdom is a gift that God has chosen to give to her, and she has used it well to encourage others.

Thanks, Mother, for the wisdom you share. Thanks for persisting all those years when I did not appreciate you. Thanks for the heritage that you and Daddy have given me. Most of all, thanks for showing by the way you have lived that, "The fear of the Lord is the beginning of wisdom" (Prv 9:10).

Crashing Cartwheels

❦

For what seemed like the millionth time, Mary Helen crashed headfirst into the ground. This time, tears welled up in her eyes. Pulling weeds out of her hair, she sat dejectedly where she had fallen, her seven-year-old body sprawled every which way. Maybe she would just give up. Soccer seemed a little less dangerous—maybe she should try that instead. Gymnastics just wasn't working out the way she had thought it would. It *looked* so easy, the way all those beautiful girls seemed to float above the ground with their flips and tucks and twists, landing perfectly on their feet every time. And here she was, failing even to master a cartwheel. Mary Helen tore at the dandelions in front of her and tossed them aside in frustration. "This is driving me crazy!" Yep, it was probably about time to take up another activity.

From the kitchen window, Mary Helen's mother Joan saw the scene unfold. As she chopped vegetables for dinner she had been watching her daughter's determined attempts to fling her small body across the front yard. It was painful to watch her youngest grow more and more discouraged. She was so close to getting it right, but every time she almost had that cartwheel, something would go wrong and she'd collapse instead. With a sigh, Joan put down her paring knife and wiped her hands on a nearby dishtowel. She tossed her apron over a chair and headed outside.

"You look kinda' tired, Mary Helen," Joan said gently, settling herself in the grass next to her daughter.

"Yeah. It's just not working. Can I quit gymnastics?"

"Are you really ready to give up on it? I've been watching from the kitchen window, and you seem like you've just about got it."

"Yeah, well, I've been close to learning stupid cartwheels for two weeks now, and everybody else has already moved on to back walkovers. I'm way behind and I'm sick of it!"

"Well, maybe you're placing your feet wrong when you start out. That could be why you keep losing your balance."

"What do you mean, placing my feet wrong? I should think I've pretty much tried everything by now! It's just me. I'm not cut out for this stuff."

"That's not true," countered Joan. "Here, watch this." And with that, she executed a perfect cartwheel. Mary Helen moaned and buried her face in her hands.

"Even *my mother* can do a cartwheel!" she wailed. "What am I, some kind of freak?!"

"Watch my feet, Mary Helen," Joan commanded, completing another. "I know you can do this!

59

C'mon, stand up and let's try some more. Pretend you're starting all over again. Here, stand by me and line up your feet like this...."

An hour and a half later, the sun set over the front yard. The half-peeled vegetables still lay by the sink, and dinner was nowhere near prepared; but Joan and Mary Helen were exultant! Dirt under their fingernails, grass in their hair, they were quite a sight when Mary Helen's father pulled into the driveway. As he climbed out of the car, Mary Helen threw herself into his arms, victorious. "Dad! Guess what! Mom taught me how to do a cartwheel! We're gonna try back walkovers tomorrow. I'm going to be the best gymnast there ever was! I can do it!"

Thanks, Mom, for taking the time to help me master those seemingly impossible tasks. Thank you for not giving up on me and for refusing to let me give up on myself.

The Gift of Caring for Others

~~~~~

little girl sat weeping on the old wooden steps of her house one day during the summer of 1875. She wept from the pain caused by rickets. But the pain in her joints couldn't compare to the pain her generation would experience. She was one of many who would live through Reconstruction, two world wars, and the Depression. Her generation lived in an era marked by difficulty.

Moosie didn't know much about her birth, only that her father had sent her pregnant mother away from Charleston to escape the Yankees who were coming to burn the city. Her mom died when Moosie was only five so she didn't remember her very well. Life was hard even then; life would *always* be hard for Moosie. Yet in the midst of her pain, seeds of a generous, caring spirit were being sown. Moosie's father, a French Huguenot, taught her that she had been blessed and that to whom much has been given, much is required, a principle known as *noblesse oblige* based on Luke 12:48.

Little Moosie grew up, married, and had children and grandchildren of her own. Along the way she developed a strength of character and an unusual determination to care for others. Just as the Great Depression began, her six-year-old granddaughter, Frances, came to live with her.

Grandmother Moosie's house was located right on Highway One which went all the way from New York to Miami. In the late twenties and early thirties there was a constant stream of hungry men hitch-hiking from New York to Miami looking for warmth and work in the South. Often a disheveled, dirty man would knock on the front door of her house seeking help.

"Frances," Grandmother Moosie would call out, "run get some soup and cornbread. We've got company."

Each time Frances scampered obediently to the kitchen and returned with bowls of okra and tomato soup, she was reminded of the importance of caring for the less fortunate. Sitting quietly there on the steps while the "traveling men" ate, Frances would listen to tales of poverty and hardship. The poor were a daily part of Frances' life because Moosie never turned anyone away.

Eventually, Frances' parents and brothers also moved into Moosie's house. They, too, joined in helping others. Every Saturday morning Frances and her brothers lined up for their "bags." Moosie had sewn three cloth bags for each child, a red one, a blue one, and a yellow one. Each bag had a drawstring so you could pull it shut easily. On Saturday Moosie gave each child three nickels, one for each of their bags. The red one was for spending, the blue bag contained the nickel for church, and the yellow one was to give to the poor.

Usually the kids made a fast trip to the corner store for an ice cream cone or some candy with their own nickel. If they were tempted to spend a nickel from their bags for the church or the poor, Moosie was quick to say, "We are so blessed. We have each other and we have a house. It's our duty in life to help others who have less than we do. It is much more important that you give to others than that you spend for yourself."

God used some of the most difficult years in our nation's history to help a lonely little girl suffering from rickets and touched by the pain of her times, to grow into a grandmother who clearly understood the Lord's commandment to care for others. Moosie taught her children and grandchildren generosity by example—and that spirit of generosity has been passed down through the generations. It has had an impact on each of Moosie's offspring. I know this because Moosie's granddaughter, Frances, is my generous mother.

Thank you, Grandmother Moosie, for living out God's command to care for others and for teaching your children and grandchildren to do the same. It is both a privilege and a challenge to learn from and to follow your God-given example.

So Many Things to Be Thankful For

~~~

others of teenagers must be the most underpaid and overworked people on the face of this earth. Sometimes it seems that words of appreciation are just not in the teenage vocabulary! I had a long chat with my dear friend, Sarah, the other day about this very thing. Sarah is fourteen and says that on the contrary, she most certainly *does* appreciate her mother! Sometimes it's just hard to express how thankful you are when you're a teenager. Sarah shared with me a great many things that she appreciates about her mother. Here's what Sarah said.

I am thankful that my mom:

- Takes the dog out at 6:00 in the morning
- Isn't afraid to race me down the street or jump on the trampoline with me
- Is always the first one to apologize
- Always notices if I pick up around the house
- Helps me give the dog a bath even though it's my dog
- Is a great Christian role model

- Is always the first to say "Hello"
- Treats everyone like she wants to be treated
- Often donates blood
- Even writes "thank you" notes for "thank you" notes!
- Will admit it when she knows she made a mistake
- Does something kind every day
- Gives the clothes our family has outgrown to charity
- Doesn't smoke
- Recycles
- Always wears a smile
- Never uses profanity
- Does daily Bible devotions
- Always asks whether I want my cocoa with or without marshmallows
- Never enters my room without knocking
- Always wears her seat belt
- Plans great family vacations
- Always has time to attend my awards banquets and recitals
- Is my hero!

Thanks, Mom, for "keeping on keeping on," even when you feel unappreciated! There are so many things I love about you, I'm just not always good at telling you so. I really do notice all the little things you do to make my life so rich. Thank you for persisting with me, even through these teenage years! I love you!

A Letter from Gramma

❦

One of my most precious possessions is a fragile piece of yellowing paper, bearing a typewritten letter and a spidery signature. It is from my husband, Will's, grandmother to me, and I cherish it as a message from her heart to mine. I know that she typed the letter because her aged fingers could not steady a pencil long enough to write. I can only imagine the painstaking time she spent perfecting the wording and spacing on a tired typewriter. Gramma's frail signature spells out both her and Granpa's names but the thoughts are all hers. They are treasures from a timeless bride to a young one. I received this gift of acceptance just a few short months before our wedding, and it brought me the peace of *belonging* when I read it. Gramma and Granpa were not able to attend our wedding because their ailing bodies could not take the chaos surrounding such an event. Even in their absence, however, we felt their blessing because of the love Gramma expressed in this letter.

Dear Allison,

Undoubtedly, the most time-consuming factor in Will's life now is you. We have observed his unfolding interest in and affection for you. We would like you to note that we have observed it and take pleasure in the decisive action he has taken in the matter. Thus, we would like to welcome you into the family circle. At the same time we would pray God's richest blessings on the home you will be establishing. May it ever affirm God's wisdom in making it a gift to his children.

We look forward to the future with excitement akin to what you must be experiencing. Suggest to Will that he help you practice saying "Gramma" and "Granpa." He has a special way of saying it.

Love,
Gramma
and
Granpa

These days, as I see Gramma struggling to conquer each new day with determination, I am still struck by her thoughtfulness in writing the letter. I was not the first young person to marry into her family, nor will I be the last. Yet she loved her grandson enough to share that love with me as well and to extend to me a special welcome into the family. I know beyond a shadow of a doubt that she is pleased with me and is happy to have me as her newest "granddaughter." For this I am very thankful.

Thank you, Gramma, for so eloquently giving me your blessing. Thank you for welcoming me with open arms into your family circle. Thank you for making such a great effort to extend to me the love you have for my husband. I am so honored to call you my "gramma"!

Wolf Repellent

❦

It seems as if all young children have fears that seem silly to grown-ups but are frighteningly real to them. When I was small, I knew for certain that there was an armed village of "little people" who lived under my bed. Of course, they only came out at night after the lights went out, so no one could ever catch them in the daytime. If I dared let a toe hang over the bedside during the night, I was sure they would rush up to it with a ladder, climb up, and chop that toe right off! The entire village would come looking for more the next night.

Fortunately, I was never unwise enough to let my toes dangle for long, and I managed to keep them from becoming a main dish. There are many other fortunate survivors among children today, courageous boys and girls who have defeated innumerable under-the-bed and in-the-closet foes. One young friend of mine was lucky enough to be rescued by his heroic mother.

Matthew had just turned six when he awoke to the realization that his home was surrounded by fierce wolves who only came out at night. They would lurk outside his bedroom window on the tree branches which scratched the side of the house, and they would sneak up the very stairs of his home, pausing to sniff and pant outside his bedroom door while he quivered under the sheets. Sometimes, he just *knew* that they had slid under his closed door and sat drooling in the shadows, breathing heavily as they waited to pounce on him the minute he fell asleep.

Matthew heroically fought the wolves by staying up all night, telling them to go away. But he was just a little boy and this could only go on for so long. At length, he admitted to his mother one day that he might need some assistance in defeating these wily foes once and for all. A brilliant woman, as all mothers of six-year-olds are, Matthew's mom had the perfect solution. After sending Matthew to the neighbor's house to play for a little while, she headed to the garage.

When Matthew returned a few hours later, he found his mother grinning victoriously. "Come see what I found, Matt!" she exclaimed, leading him to his bedroom. On his bedside table was a silver bottle, shaped oddly enough like one of Mom's hairspray bottles, but it was oh, so different! Against the bright silver glow he could see bold black letters, spelling out a word that he readily recognized. Wolf! Mom helped him with the second word, a long one that was a little bit harder to read. R-e-p-e-l-l-e-n-t. She spelled it out for him and then explained to him what it meant. Matthew shouted it at the top of his lungs. "REPELLENT! Repellent!" The words had a powerful ring to them as he said them over and over. This bottle was Matthew's secret weapon! Wolf Repellent!

Matthew's mom explained that all he had to do was spray a little bit of this magical formula in his room before he went to bed at night, and he would be wolf-free. The scent of this spray would strike fear into the heart of any and all wolves in the vicinity, and they would flee to the far ends of the earth. Matthew was guaranteed to sleep in safety. What a relief!

"Mom, you're the greatest!" Matthew cried, hugging her as tightly as he could while still holding the Wolf Repellent spray. "I promise I'll protect you and Dad from the wolves too, OK? Where did you find this stuff anyway?"

Mom just smiled and tucked a strand of fly-away hair behind her ear. "I'll never tell!" And with a grin she said, "A mom has to have some secrets, you know!"

Thanks, Mom, for taking my little fears seriously. Thank you for helping me to address them instead of ridiculing them. And thank you for your creativity in finding solutions to them!

No Expectations

"So, has it been a good summer so far?" Mom asked, anxious to catch up on the past two months of her daughter's life. Letters from camp had been few and far between, but now Lynn was home for a quick weekend off.

"It's been great for the most part, Mom, but I'm ready for it to be over! I don't know what on earth possessed me to agree to three full summer terms. I ran out of energy about ten days ago, and since then I have just been running on sheer determination."

Lynn sighed, "I'm having trouble loving the kids...in fact, some days I don't even *like* them, and the only thing that keeps me going is my sense of obligation to them! I get so tired of trying to be enthusiastic about games and songs and silly competitions! I'm sick of breaking up arguments, dealing with the raging hormones of a dozen teenage girls, and reminding them to keep the cabin tidy. They are so self-centered and unappreciative!

"I feel like I give and give and give with no return and no thanks. I'm just given out. I really don't think I can go back to camp on Sunday. I'll go crazy—I'll just crack! I can't do it anymore, and even though there are only a few weeks left, I think I'm going to call and resign early. They'll survive without me. Nobody seems to notice anything I do anyway!"

Lynn's mother sat quietly as she listened to her discouraged daughter. She certainly knew what it was to feel exhausted and unappreciated. She had raised five children, after all! She wanted to boost Lynn's spirits but also to challenge her not to give up. How well she understood her daughter's feelings....

"Lynn, I am so proud of you!" she began slowly. "You have worked so hard this summer—much harder than you expected to, I am sure. You are a wonderful, godly role model for those young girls, and although they may not always act like it, I am sure they love and appreciate you. I know what you mean about feeling like you are working for nothing, though. So often in life we feel like no one really recognizes the value of the love and labor we keep on giving."

Lynn nodded in agreement with her mother. *That's exactly how I feel,* she thought to herself.

"If there is one thing I have learned as a mother, though, it is this: *Sometimes in life you have to give without expecting to receive.* Children, whether they are your own or campers at Bluestone, are not always going to recognize and appreciate all that you do for them. Those girls don't realize the sacrifices you have made to be there with them this summer, and they won't necessarily appreciate the fact

75

that you have given every last ounce of energy you have for their sakes. Even so, that does not lessen the importance of what you are doing. You are making an impact on those young lives. Don't give up! I have some great Scripture verses that I encourage myself with whenever I'm feeling unappreciated. Maybe it will help you to keep them in mind. Colossians 3:23 and 24 say: 'Whatever you do, work at it with all your heart, as working for the Lord, not for men, [or for teenage girls!] since you know that you will receive an inheritance from the Lord as a reward. It is the Lord Christ you are serving.'

"Keep in mind, Sweetheart, that your heavenly Father sees and values the efforts you make to care for these campers. He sees your exhaustion, he knows your frustrations, and he is proud of you. He appreciates the work that you do, so remember that when you have to settle teenage disputes, you are doing it for the Lord as well as for those girls. When you teach them a new game, you are serving the Lord, even as you do when you pray with them. All of your efforts are not in vain—they are seen and appreciated by the one whose opinion matters the most. And I love you and I am proud of you, too. Now, let's get your bags packed up so you can get back to camp!"

✿

Thanks, Mom, for all those years of being unappreciated. I can never begin to thank you for all that you have done for me, but know that I value you and all that you gave of yourself to help me grow. Thank you for teaching me to give without expecting to receive anything tangible in return. Thank you for pointing me to my Creator and reminding me that he sees all and that I can do everything in his name. His pleasure in me is the greatest reward. Thank you for reminding me of this and for not letting me give in to my discouragement!

✿

Making the Best of a Painful Situation

❧

I leaned heavily against the front door to close it and shut out the frosty stillness of the December night. A stately Norwegian pine, its boughs laden with green lights and gold balls, presided over our decorations. The warmth and beauty of our Christmasy living room made me feel wrapped in love. Scented candles graced the perimeter of the room, their flames filling the space with quiet light.

I dropped my burden of firewood on the hearth and began to crumple newspaper for kindling. Making the fire on Christmas Eve had always been Dad's job. But now that Mom and Dad were divorced, that responsibility, like many others, fell on me. At sixteen I considered myself quite capable of handling an adult role. My two sisters, ages seven and thirteen, were helping Mom make appetizers in the kitchen.

"Ann," my mother called from the kitchen, "don't forget to open the damper before you light the fire."

She always reminded me of this, since once, long ago, I'd forgotten and turned our Christmas Eve celebration into a smoky mess!

"Don't worry, Mom!" I responded while busily trying to get the fire lit before Dad arrived. Just as the blaze caught, I heard his heavy pounding at the front door.

"Hey daughters, I'm here!" he cheerfully called out as he came in laden with packages. Immediately he was surrounded by three girls fairly bursting with excitement. Then we remembered Mom. We turned to look at her. Her eyes, brimming with tears, met Dad's and they exchanged Christmas greetings. She smiled a hurt, painful smile, and the awkwardness lifted. Dad hurried upstairs to wrap our presents and Christmas was under way. For one night of the year, we were a real family again.

Growing up in a broken family is painful and holidays can be especially hard. At holiday time there's so much emphasis on family togetherness and, well, our family wasn't together. Two years earlier Dad had walked out on Mom and us girls. There were tears, there was confusion, there were so many *whys?* screaming for answers to wash away the pain. But there weren't any answers. It was a painful situation, full of heartache, with no easy solution.

But my mother made a choice, and with that choice she gave us an example of one of life's greatest lessons. Instead of choosing to sink into self-pity and bitterness, she chose to make the best of a difficult situation.

Until Dad remarried he came back to our home each year for Christmas Eve. Mom asked him to. She wanted him there for us girls. I'm sure it was hard for her, but she determined not to let her personal wounds make her bitter. Even though she had divorced, Mom taught us that God hates divorce. Our family knew, first hand, the pain of divorce, and she instilled in each of us girls the desire for a marriage that would last.

Later, when my husband and I struggled in our own marriage, Mom encouraged us to work it out. She reminded us to make our marriage the most important priority after our relationship with God. When I told her I found it easier to focus on my children, Mom said, "Ann, put your husband first. Your marriage is the most important thing in your life, and if you put your husband first, your children will be blessed. Spend time with him in the evenings. Develop good communication skills. Read good books on marriage. Work at it. Because you did not have good role models, you will have to work extra hard. But your marriage is worth all the work. As your children watch you, they, too, will learn that marriage takes work, and they, too, will be willing to work on their own marriages. You are building for the future."

Thanks, Mom, for making the choice to see the positive side of a difficult situation. You refused to become bitter or to quit. Instead, you demonstrated for me and my sisters that God can use a painful situation if we choose to trust him and look for the good. You have inspired us to work through the tough times in our own marriages, and you have enabled us to have close relationships with you and with our dad.

It's Never Too Late

༃༄

Mum's bent frame leaned over her bowl of cereal. As she reached for her spoon with spotted, wrinkled hands she said, "You know, Audrey, I'm the only one who doesn't take *it*. I really think it's too late now."

What? Audrey thought. Then, all of a sudden Audrey realized that her Mum wasn't talking about toast and marmalade. No, she was talking about the communion service held monthly at her retirement home. Her mother was lamenting the fact that she did not feel she could receive communion.

Hope raced through Audrey's heart. Could this be the answer to her prayers of so many years? Was her mother really expressing an interest in knowing God?

For more than ten years Audrey had prayed daily for her mother to come to know Christ in a personal way. She had shared with Mum her own spiritual journey, the changes Christ had brought about in her own life, and her longing for her mother to know Christ as she did. But until this moment, Mum had been unreceptive.

Mum had lived through two world wars and a depression. As a young woman she was strikingly beautiful and very witty. She was also extremely bright and an avid reader. She developed into a woman of authority with unusual organizational abilities. Her marriage broke up when Audrey was three, and Mum was forced by circumstances to develop her own business. She managed apartments to provide support for herself and her daughter. Even though the times were difficult, she maintained a positive outlook on life and viewed her challenges with a sense of adventure rather than despair. She believed in God but just couldn't conceive that Jesus was his Son or believe that there was actually a heaven.

Because Audrey was an only child, she was especially close to her mother. When she married, however, Audrey and her husband lived in the States while Mum remained in England. Audrey went often to England to care for Mum. The last year had been especially hard. At eighty-six, Mum's health began to deteriorate rapidly, and Audrey found herself wondering if her prayers for her mother's salvation would ever be answered. Several close calls increased Audrey's anxiety, and she pleaded, "Lord, please help Mum know you, and let me be with her when she dies." But still Audrey's doubts whispered, *It's getting rather late for her to change.*

Yet now, at this very moment, Mum seemed to be opening the door! With a fresh sense of hope, Audrey responded, "Oh Mum, it's not too late. Why don't I call the minister and ask him to talk with us about this."

With Mum's permission, Audrey phoned the Anglican minister who held the services in the retirement home. He was happy to begin a private instruction class to prepare Mum for baptism and confirmation. He was undaunted by her age and physical limitations. Through his gentle explanations of the love of Christ, Mum's old eyes opened with a new understanding of his deity and of his promise of eternal life.

In June Mum was confirmed by the Bishop of Taunton. To celebrate, Audrey gave Mum a wonderful private party in her room with strawberries and cream. She presented her mother with a simple gold cross on a chain. Mum would have thought the gift silly just a few months earlier, but now she put it on with pride and told her nurse, "See my cross. It's new today!"

Three months later, as Audrey sat on the bed holding her mother up in a sitting position to help her breathe more easily, Mum slipped quietly away. She died in Audrey's arms. Overwhelmed with emotion, Audrey whispered, "Oh God, you have given me more than I could ask or imagine. It *wasn't* too late for Mum."

Then, as Audrey held Mum close, the sun burst through the window, and it seemed as if the room was filled with golden angels who had come to take Mum home.

Thank you, Mum, for reminding me that it is never too late to come to God. Thank you for allowing him to put his arms around you, assuring you of eternal life and, in the process, reminding me that God is faithful and he is never too late.

Curtains and a Labor of Love

❧

When Will and I were newly married, we had a little bit of "in-between time" before we left to move into our new home in Florida. So, for a month we were given the privilege and the challenge of living with our parents. We spent a few nights at my parents', then a few nights at his, and back and forth we went. Now, don't get me wrong. We really love our families and were thankful for the extra time with them before we moved away to start our new life together. However, sometimes even family can be a little too close for comfort!

When we walked into Will's home after our honeymoon, we were greeted with hugs and welcoming smiles, and I felt surprisingly comfortable with my new role as an "official" member of the family. For some reason, I had expected to feel uncomfortable. I don't know why. At any rate, I felt completely at ease... until the evening passed by and it was getting close to bedtime. I suddenly began to have twinges of fear in my tummy. "Oh my goodness! We're actually going to have to sleep together under Will's parents' roof!" The thought hit me like a bolt of lightning, and my feelings of ease faded quickly into nervousness. I was having a hard enough time getting used to sleeping with another body in my bed, and I didn't know if I could make it through the night knowing that we were surrounded by that body's family! That was just a little too weird for me. To make matters worse, we had to sleep in the family room on the sofa bed where everyone came to watch early-morning cartoons! Heaven forbid that Will's family find out we were sleeping together! I tried to reassure myself that this was no big deal. *Married people usually do sleep in the same bed, you know,* I thought to myself. But I was still feeling uncomfortable about it.

As I was brushing my teeth in the downstairs bathroom, I saw out of the corner of my eye that Will's mom was coming down the stairs. I thought she had gone to bed. What could she be up to? Checking up on us? I was so disconcerted I brushed my cheek, accidentally! She had a huge bundle in her arms and was trying not to drop some long rods. *What on earth...?* I wondered, giving up on my toothbrush. I kept watching her, this time in the mirror's reflection. She was unfolding some cloth on the kitchen table, and it looked like long curtains. I tossed my toothbrush on the sink and went into the kitchen to see what was going on.

"I made you some curtains," she said with a shy grin. "I thought we could hang them in the doorway to the family room so that you could have a little bit of privacy." My jaw went slack with surprise. "We are so glad you are here with us, and I thought this might make you newlyweds feel a little more comfortable." Had she been reading my mind or something? I laughed sheepishly and gave my new mom a big hug. This was one smart woman! As I helped her put the curtain rods above the doorway, I realized that this had been no small task. Will's mom had gone to a great deal of trouble to make a private space for us in her home.

As Will and I snuggled behind our curtains that night, I couldn't help but laugh at myself. What a small thing a set of curtains is, but what a big difference it can make!

Thanks, Mom, for those curtains you made me! Thank you for your thoughtfulness in recognizing my need for a little bit of privacy even before I did and for the hard work that you put into providing them. Thank you for sharing your son with me and for the thoughtful ways you have shown me that you are glad we married.

An Ever-Faithful Fan

❦

hadows were creeping across the infield as Nate grabbed his glove and trotted out to his short-stop position. The chill of an early fall sent shivers up his spine reminding him that he really preferred *spring* baseball. But his school played in the fall, and he loved it too much to give it up. Throwing a warm-up grounder to the first baseman, Nate glanced at the stands to see if she had arrived yet. Not yet, and, looking up, he paused for a moment and silently whispered, "Lord, help her get here safely."

It was another long trip for Nate's mom. She had nearly a two-hour drive out of the city in rush hour traffic to get to his game. She would be tired, too, having spent the whole day at work downtown, and she probably wouldn't have taken time to eat.

Life hadn't been easy for Nate's mom, Anna. Growing up poor in the coal mine region of Virginia, she was one of seven children. When she was only five years old she watched her beloved papa die of black lung disease. Her earliest memories were of waiting in line for free cheese in the government subsidies program and of helping her exhausted mother care for her siblings. When she finished high school she left the security of her rural community to venture all by herself to Washington, D.C. She was determined to find a job that would enable her to help her family.

A job, a happy marriage, and two wonderful children brought Anna much joy and a new sense of security. But then her world fell apart. Her husband announced that he was leaving. There was someone else. Nate was only eight and his sister ten when their father left. The emotional pain was tremendous, finances were tight, and each day was a struggle. But Anna did what she had to do. She worked hard, and she was there for her kids. School shows, ball games—every one was important to her.

"Why, Mom's probably been to a hundred baseball games, a hundred tennis matches, and two hundred basketball games," Nate mused. "And the amazing thing is that she is not an athlete. In fact, she still doesn't understand tennis. She doesn't put pressure on me or try to coach me. She's just there for me. After Dad left, Mom made an extra effort to be there. With so much instability in our lives, her presence gave me a sense of security."

Turning his thoughts back to the game at hand, Nate realized that tonight it was really going to be cold before the game ended. And it would probably be close to midnight before they got home. His mom would have to get up early to fix breakfast, get the kids to the bus, and catch the metro for work in the city. Not much sleep and another long day tomorrow.

Just as the first inning finished he saw her, wrapped in a blanket sitting on the hard metal bleacher. Only three other parents had bothered to come. It wasn't an important game. It was cold, a long way from home, and already late. But she was there. She saw Nate's anxious look and waved her hand in reassurance. And once again his heart soared with the knowledge of her presence.

Thank you, Mom, for being there. Even when it was hard and you were tired and you didn't even understand the sport, you came. You were there and your presence has given me comfort, security, and confidence. Your presence has given me a better understanding of God's presence. I know that he will always be there for me— even when you are no longer able to be.

White House Dinners

❦

W hen you were growing up, did your parents always tell you to sit up straight at the table, take off your hat when you are inside, and always to wash your hands before dinner? Mine certainly did! Mom was the expert because she taught us what to do and what not to do, but we didn't appreciate the learning process very much at that time!

Thursday nights were family nights in our household. We all had to be home for dinner no matter what. Baseball games, cheerleading practice, and church meetings were no excuse. You were there, *or else*! On those nights we often had what Mom loved to call "White House Dinners." No, our house was not white. In fact, it was red brick, and we lived on Broadmont Terrace instead of Pennsylvania Avenue. But on Thursdays, it didn't matter where we were because we were eating at the White House. Mr. and Mrs. President never could make it to join us, but Mom and Dad stood in for them pretty well. Mom always argued that, "You just never know when you might get invited someplace special for dinner. When you do, you'll be glad I taught you how to behave!"

There were many rules that we had to abide by at

those White House Dinners. Mom always cooked a "fancy" meal and we set the table with the fine china, silver, and cloth napkins. We ate in the dining room instead of the kitchen, and Mom and Dad debated over just how dim the lights should be to get maximum "atmosphere" from the candles, while still allowing us to see the food on our plates! We all had to dress nicely for dinner, or at least put on a clean shirt and wash our faces. Mom always wore fresh lipstick, and Dad smelled good. We sat patiently at the table with our hands in our laps until Dad blessed the food (and he took an extra long time on Thursdays), thanked Mom for cooking such a lovely dinner, and began to serve the meal. We passed everything to our right, served the person sitting next to us, took care to drop a little to the dog without letting Mom catch us, chewed with our mouths shut and made sure our napkins were in our laps. If our elbows happened to graze the tablecloth, Mom would burst out in a rousing rendition of "Mabel, Mabel, strong and able, get your elbows off the table!", and we were sure to have dish duty that night!

Mastering the intricacies of which spoon to use for soup and which for dessert, which knife belonged with the butter, and where to place your fork when you were finished was a complicated task requiring many, many Thursday nights practicing at the White House. When it finally came time to clear the table, we were carefully instructed to ask politely, "Have you finished?" instead of "Are ya' done?" (Only turkeys get "done," you know!), and we were cautioned against the greatest dinner *faux pas* of them all—stacking dishes at the table! Of course, even after everyone had finished eating, our favorite television shows were well over, and we were all paralyzed from sitting up straight for so long, we *still* had to sit and make nice conversation while Mom and Dad drank bottomless cups of coffee. That was pure torture. Not even a telephone call was permitted to interrupt Mom's perfect White House Dinners. We ate with the answering machine on, without fail.

After months and months of White House Dinners, Mom decided that it was time to put us to the test. We would go out to a nice restaurant and see how well we could perform! Now, to us kids, this seemed like a much more reasonable way to learn manners than at home *pretending* we were at the White House. We figured the first family never had time for fancy dinners together anyway! So, we traipsed happily to the local Chinese restaurant where we sat up tall, said "Please," "Thank You," and "Please pass the soy sauce" to perfection. Mom was definitely proud. She couldn't help but give us a few very specific reminders, though. Just as she was proclaiming vehemently in her not-so-quiet voice, "And remember, never, *ever* stack your plates. It's *so* rude!" our waiter, laden with a pile of dishes he had collected from another table, stepped up and asked, "Are ya' done? Can I stack your plates?" We all roared with laughter.

It took a few years and many more White House Dinners until we convinced Mom that we were sufficiently educated on manners. We were prepared for any glamorous occasion that might arise, and not too long ago, one actually did. We were all invited to the White House, the real one this time, for a holiday dinner party! And you know what? Thanks to Mom, we knew exactly what to do!

Thanks, Mom, for teaching us the finer things in life! We are comfortable in so many situations because you taught us how to behave as "ladies" and "gentlemen." We did get tired of your endless lectures on how to be polite, but we are grateful for your ceaseless efforts to refine us. We hope to always make you proud!

A Glimpse of Eternity

❦

My mother suffered from depression. As a result, during much of my life, I was her emotional caretaker. I somehow understood at an early age that, not only was it important to be emotionally self-sufficient, but it was also my role to be for Mom whatever she needed me to be. I was her encourager and her confidante. In a way, I was the parent and she was the child.

When Mom was seventy-five she learned that she had malignant tumors in her neck and chest that had spread from a cancer she'd had treated three years before. This time the doctors told us that she had approximately six months to live. Mom believed in God and had asked Jesus to be her Lord and Savior. Intellectually, she knew she was redeemed, forgiven, and loved, but it was difficult for her to experience the reality of a loving Father on a daily basis.

Fervently my brother, sisters, and I prayed that God would be merciful to our mother. During this time I had also been praying that I would feel the love and presence of God in my life in a fresh way. The support structure of my faith was strong and solid, but I had been longing to feel and experience in a *new* way what I believed and knew to be the truth of the gospel. God answered this prayer through my relationship with my mother.

During the last month of Mother's life I was able to go to be with her for three days. When it was time for me to leave her at the end of this visit, knowing that it would likely be the last time I'd see her before she died, I fell apart. I simply could no longer contain my tears or my pain, nor could I hide them from her. I held on to her like a small child would, sobbing. "I can't do this; it's just too hard for me. I can't leave you," I cried.

Mother, on the other hand, was peaceful and composed for the first time in my life. She comforted me. She told me that she loved me and was proud of me. She became for me the strong, capable mother that I had never known. There was such healing in those moments. I felt like I was given a glimpse of Mother in eternity—whole and emotionally and physically released from the disabilities that had so confined her during this life. I experienced what felt like a pure mother and daughter relationship, in which I was the daughter instead of the mother. And I sensed strongly and clearly the love and presence of God. God was very merciful to both my mother and to me. He gave me back my mother and he gave me a glimpse of the wholeness of eternal life with him.

Thank you, Mother, for doing the best you could. Thank you, God, for giving me a real mother at the end but most of all for giving me a glimpse of the wholeness we have to look forward to in eternal life with you.

Will You Please Forgive Me?

❦

I t was a "grouchy Saturday morning" because Mom was in a bad mood, and whenever Mom was tired, cranky, or not feeling well, everyone was grouchy and we kids just seemed to get in a lot more trouble than usual. I'm not even sure what happened on this particular day, but as a mischievous little six-year-old, I must have done something to set Mom off. She gave me the scolding of my life, and I ran crying to my room.

About forty-five minutes later, after I had cried out my tears and moved on to more interesting things, Mom called me to come out of my room and downstairs. Her tremulous voice reminded me that I had been in trouble, so I crept as quietly down the stairs as I could, hoping not to set her temper off again by being too noisy. As I rounded the curve at the bottom of the stairs, I saw Mom sitting there waiting for me. I wondered if I was in trouble again. It often happened that I was in trouble without quite realizing why! Mom did not look very happy, so I assumed I had done it again. "What did I do this time, Mommy?" I asked timidly. To my surprise,

99

Mom said nothing but burst into tears! I started to cry, too, thinking that I had *really* blown it this time. What could I have done?

"Oh, Sweetheart," she said, "you didn't do anything! I'm just crying because I feel like a bad mommy. I lost my temper earlier and took it out on you. I should not have done that, but sometimes mommies make mistakes. I'm so sorry. Will you please forgive me?"

"YES!" I said, eager to please my teary mother. I gave her a big hug. Then I realized I didn't understand. "Mommy? What does it mean to forgive?"

A smile broke through the tears rolling down her cheeks, and she said, "It means not to be angry anymore when somebody hurts your feelings or does something mean. It means you tell them, 'It's OK—I still love you, and I'll forget about it.'"

Oh... this began to make sense to my young mind. "Like Jesus did when those people hurt him and killed him and he still loved them?"

"Yes, exactly like that, Sweetie," she said. "Jesus is the best forgiver in the world. Sometimes it's hard for normal people like us to forgive. And you know what's sometimes even harder?"

"What, Mommy?"

"*Asking* someone to forgive you. You know what I was doing while you were up in your room? I was sitting down here arguing with myself. You see, I knew in my heart that I was ugly to you earlier. But I kept thinking 'Oh well. Mothers are like that sometimes.' I was making up excuses for myself, when I really needed to say I was sorry and ask you to forgive me."

"So, sometimes you have to say 'Sorry' and 'Will you please forgive me' at the same time?"

"Yes, you certainly do!" Mom replied and gave me a big bear hug. "Thank you for forgiving me. I love you!"

"You're welcome, Mommy. I love you too, and I forgive you forever!"

⚜

Thanks, Mom, for teaching me that sometimes "Sorry" is not enough. It is so hard to ask for forgiveness, especially from the people we love most. I will never forget the day you taught me the importance of those words, "Will you please forgive me?" The best thing about this little phrase is that it demands a response. It brings humility and closure to those hurtful moments, when a less sincere "Sorry," flung in passing, would not be enough to heal the wounds or bind up a broken relationship.

⚜

A Most Unusual Dime Collection

❧

M y brother Doug, Mom, and I were sitting, knees curled up at the kitchen table, enjoying one of those late night snacks. There had been company at our house earlier, but everyone had gone home and we could finally relax.

With a big grin on her face, Mom reached into her pocket and pulled out a fistful of dimes. Dumping them into the center of the table she turned to me. "Sandra, I saw you talking to old Mr. Wells tonight. Tell us about your time with him."

My first thought was how boring Mr. Wells had been, but then a glance at the shiny dimes inspired me to say, "Well, I learned all about fly fishing from him. He really knows about lures and fishing. I guess you could say he's a fishing expert."

"Wow, I didn't know that about Mr. Wells. How fascinating!" Mom responded, pushing a dime toward me.

Doug and Dad soon joined in as we compared notes on the evening and the people we had talked with. Most of the dimes soon disappeared, although a few had to be returned to the pile during the conversation. Mom had invented her dime game when we were very small to teach us to look for something good in each person. Whenever we paid a genuine positive compliment about someone, we were allowed to take a dime, but if we made a negative remark about a person we had to *give* a dime.

Throughout her life, Mom always seemed to make conscious choices to be positive. On another occasion when we were small I saw a blouse I desperately wanted. And Doug was dying for a basketball. But finances were tight, and Mom couldn't afford either. As we discussed this one morning, Mom said, "I know what we *can* afford! Let's go get sundaes!" Marching up to the counter at the ice cream shop Mom put her money on the counter and exclaimed, "There are three of us, give us the works!"

Over hot fudge sundaes topped with nuts and whipped cream we told jokes and laughed. And Mom said, "Well, we don't have a basketball, and we don't have a new blouse, but we have each other and we sure have fun."

Another time Mom decided one of Dad's office parties was going to be too staid, so she dressed up in crazy clothes and pranced into the room, guitar in hand singing, "You ain't nothing but a hound dog." Soon the whole staff was relaxed and laughing.

But when she was forty-three we began to notice a change in Mom. She seemed distracted and couldn't concentrate. And she couldn't remember things. One day at the grocery store she signed "Mickey Mouse" to her check.

"Why did you do that?" I asked later.

"I couldn't remember my name and I didn't want them to know," she responded in one of her clearer moments.

Not much was known about Alzheimers disease in those days, but that's what Mom had. Seven long, hard years followed before she died. By that time my brother and I were in our teens. The time we spent with Mom was too brief. But today when I think of her, I'm so grateful for the lessons she packed into those short years.

Thanks, Mom, for teaching us to look for the good in every person and in every situation. Thanks for showing us how to approach life with a positive spirit and a sense of fun rather than with self-pity. My pile of dimes grows higher each time I think of you.

Big Heart, Open Door

rowing up I didn't think my life was very unusual or appreciate how special my mother was. Now, as an adult looking back, the fact that I didn't realize my youth was unusual is a tribute in itself.

I was the oldest of seven kids in a busy household. But that was just the beginning of busyness! One night when I was still young, the doorbell rang. Standing on our front steps were my aunt and her six kids. All of them had long faces and heavy suitcases. A difficult marriage had forced them to flee to our home. We certainly hadn't been expecting them, but Mom wasn't fazed one bit!

"Come on in!" she exclaimed. "Isn't this great? Christine," she called to me, "get out the ice cream and let's have a party." We unpacked suitcases and found extra pillows. Our cousins climbed into bed with us. This one-night sleepover turned into a year's stay.

A few years later, two young Vietnamese girls who had fled Vietnam on a flimsy boat came to live with us. Mom said, "We can share with them. They have no family and don't speak a word of English. They need us."

Then later, a foster child—a darling little girl of

five—arrived for a year. Linda had many special needs.

But the end was not yet in sight. My dad's sister died suddenly of a brain tumor. Her husband had long before deserted her and their children. Her kids were left with no one. Three of her children came to live with us and my mom and dad raised them, too! At one point Mom and Dad had seven teenagers living at home. Particularly challenging were three boys—all aged sixteen and all getting their driving permits in the same year!

We weren't wealthy, but Mom was a "stretcher." Spaghetti stretched to feed ten hungry children. At dinnertime chairs were gathered from all around the house so that we could eat together. Sharing was nothing new in our house! We'd always had to share. If we refused to share, the item in dispute was taken away. If we shared and our toy was broken by someone else it was always replaced by Mom or Dad. Everyone living at our house always pitched in to help with chores. Extra kids meant extra workers!

I can't remember Mom ever complaining or feeling sorry for herself. Instead, she looked at life as an adventure. Her big heart just kept expanding to enfold whomever God brought to our home.

I never felt slighted or neglected as our family grew. There was too much happy confusion to feel slight or neglect. Caring for those in need never seemed unusual to me. I assumed everyone was like my mom!

I didn't fully appreciate my mother's impact upon me until recently when a friend commented, "Christine, your mother, Marjorie, is amazing. I don't know how she did it—taking in and raising so many kids. But hearing about her and learning how you grew up helps me understand you better. Look at the many young people you have taken in to live with you. You've inherited your mother's big heart and her open door."

"Why," I replied with surprise, "I guess I have and I didn't even realize it! It just seemed so natural to me."

Thank you, Mom, for living with a big heart and an open door and for handing down the legacy to me.

A Worthy Investment
༼ེ༽

W hen we were growing up we always sus-
pected our mother was a little bit crazy.
Now that we're older, she seems to
have regained most of her senses, but for awhile we
wondered about her! One day in particular stands
out in my mind. I really questioned her sanity. It
was a Saturday afternoon in the fall and Mom had
been running errands all day. We five kids were rak-
ing leaves in the front yard when Mom pulled into
the driveway. She was driving our beat-up old
pickup truck. (It still amazes me that she wasn't
embarrassed to be seen in that thing.) As she leaped
out of the truck, I noticed something in the bed.

"Hey kids, come see what I got!" Mom yelled
excitedly, and we rushed over to investigate. We
never knew what Mom would be up to. She climbed
up into the back of the truck, flung her arms open
wide, and cried, "Ta Daa! Can you believe it was
free?" She wore an enormous smile of anticipation.

Climbing into the pickup to join her, we saw the
ugliest couch in the world. It had once been blue
and red plaid, but now it was faded, stained, and the
stuffing was coming out in spots.

"Mother, please tell me you're not putting this in
the living room!" I groaned, dreading the embarrass-

ment of explaining this monstrosity to my friends. Teenage boys were supposed to pull stunts like this, not mothers! Sometimes Mom was just nuts.

"Of course not!" Mom laughed and began to explain. "I'm going to put it in the garage. You see, I had this idea that we could clean out the garage a little bit and make it into a kids' hangout room. Mr. Larson down the street said we could have his old Ping-Pong table for only ten dollars if we wanted it, and we'll set that up in there too. Then, when friends come over you can hang out in the garage, stay up late, and not bother anybody! So what do you think?"

I looked at my brothers and sisters, who were obviously excited by the idea. "Hooray!" Chris yelled. "It can be a guys-only hangout. No girls allowed. Right John?" John was quick to agree, but Mom interrupted as my sisters and I began to protest.

"We'll all share it. You know that's how we do things around here! But before we do anything else, we've got to get that garage cleaned out. Let's go!" Rakes and leaf piles were deserted as we followed Mom to the garage. I had to admit, as crazy as Mom was to bring home a nasty couch, the idea of a hangout room was starting to grow on me. There was already a basketball hoop and a dartboard outside the garage. This could actually become a pretty cool place to hang out. I wasn't so sure my girlfriends were into Ping-Pong, but at least we could sit on the couch (once I found a *clean* blanket to cover those spots) and talk.

Our garage quickly became a neighborhood favorite where kids in the neighborhood could hang out and relax. Mom could not have been happier. She *loved* having lots of young people around the house. They all loved her too and treated her like one of the gang. Sometimes I would come home at night with friends and end up going to bed while Mom and my friends were still sitting up chatting! Everyone considered her their friend, and I was secretly very proud of having a "cool" mom.

Mom made our house a place that was always open to our friends, no matter who they were or what their background and reputation were. She loved everybody! Our parents were always very strict about our going out at night to parties and on dates, but Mom was always quick to remind us that she was glad to have all our friends come to *our* house. We could always bring the party home! Her real concern was that we were safe. She was much happier knowing that the party was going on downstairs instead of somewhere else! I think that Mom and Dad probably passed many sleepless hours, while Ping-Pong games and basketball tournaments went on outside their bedroom window at all hours of the night. But we never once heard them complain. To them, it was a worthwhile sacrifice.

Mom wasn't the kind of mother who always had cookies and milk waiting for us and our friends.

Instead she had refrigerated cookie dough, brownie mixes, and microwave popcorn available twenty-four hours a day! Even now, when my husband and I come to visit my parents, we can count on seeing my brothers and sisters and friends there in the kitchen! Sometimes, even when my siblings aren't there, their friends are! Mom has so endeared herself to them by her open heart and open house policy, they know they can count on her to listen when no one else will. She made our home into one of love and acceptance for anyone who walked in our front door. Oh, by the way, we still have that old couch in the garage, too. It's pretty much destroyed, but it's a very special monument to Mom's investment in our lives and our relationships.

Thanks, Mom, for making our home into a place where all our friends feel welcome! Thank you for understanding our adolescent need to be surrounded by peers and for giving up your garage (and ultimately the rest of your house!) to that end. Thank you for feeding our friends, for listening to them, and for treating them with respect. It is such a good feeling to know that our home has been, and will continue to be, a place where our friends feel loved. It gives us great pleasure to share you with others. We are so proud you are our mom!

She Gave Me Hope

ears streamed down Gail's face as she clutched the phone tightly in her hand. Her throbbing face had already begun to swell from the beating, and her shoulder ached with bruises from her father's grip. Hiding in the dark corner of the room with the phone, she listened in panic as again the ring went unanswered. Finally a voice said "Hello" and Gail began to weep.

"Iva Lee, it's me," she sobbed. "My father beat me up again, this time because I didn't finish the ironing and I couldn't keep the baby from crying. He says I can't do anything right. He says I'm awful!"

Gail's sobs increased as she poured out her broken heart to Iva Lee. Once again Iva listened to Gail's pain and did her best to comfort her. "You are not awful. You are dear and precious. You must have hope and count the days, Gail. You're nearly eighteen! You'll be able to leave soon. God loves you and he does have a future for you. You *will* make it."

Once again Iva Lee prayed for Gail on the phone before she hung up. This wasn't Gail's first panic call to her Sunday school teacher and it wouldn't be the last. Each time Iva Lee listened and comforted. And she never hung up without praying for Gail on the phone. At this time, there was little recognition or recourse for domestic violence. Because of this, Iva Lee's ability to change Gail's circumstances was limited.

Gail's home life was miserable. Her parents were divorced and she lived mainly with her father and stepmother. By the time Gail graduated from high school they had moved twenty times to avoid custody battles.

Gail's father ruled their home with fear. Even as a young teen, Gail was responsible for cooking, cleaning, and taking care of two small siblings. When she failed to do things to his satisfaction, Gail's father would grab his belt and the beatings would begin again.

The belt came out at other times, too, like the time he was determined that she learn to do a back dive. He stood by the diving board with his belt and hit her until she got it right.

For Gail, religion was distorted with fear as well. At one point the family joined a religious community which insisted upon unreasonably strict rules and perpetuated a faith based on fear. Gail was told she was controlled by demons and that she needed punishing.

The one "outsider" Gail's father liked was Iva Lee. He let Gail spend time with her, encouraging her to go to a summer Bible camp that Iva Lee arranged for. And Iva Lee was careful not to antagonize him lest he forbid Gail to spend time with her.

Iva Lee was a busy mother with three small

children. Yet she eagerly came alongside Gail and acted as a mother to her. Iva Lee shared with Gail a God of love, not fear. She prayed for her daily. And she spent time with her. She talked with her over and over again on the phone, patiently enduring emergency calls that came at 2:00 A.M.

From Iva Lee, Gail began to learn of a God who loved her and in whom she could hope. The day she turned eighteen, Gail did leave home. The pain wasn't over, but she had survived and she had a sense that in spite of everything God loved her.

Perhaps most amazing of all was Iva Lee's impact on Gail's relationship with her father. Gail easily could have been overcome with hate. Instead, with Iva Lee's encouragement, she developed compassion and realized that her father had not intended to do evil to her. His own abusive background had not prepared him for the challenges of parenting. And though he should have paid for his crimes with time in prison, Gail was able to give her father forgiveness and love. In his last days before he died, Gail was with him, and they were able to speak of the few good times they had experienced together.

The prayers and friendship of an older woman had enabled a desperate teenager to cling to a God of hope. And God did not disappoint.

Thank you, Iva Lee, for loving me when I thought I was unlovable, for giving hope where there was only despair, and for pointing me to a compassionate heavenly Father who promised, "For I know the plans I have for you...plans to prosper you and not to harm you, plans to give you a hope and a future" (Jer 29:11). Thank you, Father, for giving this abused child a hope and a future.

Teach Me to Pray

❧✦❧

I distinctly remember waking up in the night as a child and hearing the sound of my little brother's voice in the next room. He was talking to someone, but at first I couldn't quite determine to *whom*. Who in the world would be in there chatting with him in the middle of the night? As I listened more, I realized that although John prattled on, no one was responding. I crept to my bedroom door and leaned out into the hallway so I could hear better. Then I realized there was no one else in the room with him. He was praying! I heard his sincere little voice continue on, "And Jesus, let her love animals and bikes, run really fast, but not as fast as me, and look like my mommy. And especially let her have smooth hair. Amen".

Smooth hair? What was my little brother talking about? I laughed to myself, climbed back into bed, and fell asleep chuckling. When I asked John about it the next day, he calmly explained that he had awakened in the middle of the night. And no, he wasn't scared. He was *much* too big to be scared, but he couldn't fall asleep. So, he did what Mom always told us to do when we couldn't fall asleep. He prayed.

"And just what were you praying about so hard,

John?" I questioned. He gave a big smile and replied with satisfaction, "My wife!" I did a double take and had to bite my tongue to keep from laughing out loud. Being a mature ten-year-old, I was concerned about such things, but what was a mere child of eight doing thinking about his future mate?

"Mom told me that it's important to pray for the girl I want to marry!" John quickly explained. "I mean, pray for her now and every day so that she'll be ready for me when I finally meet her! You better do the same thing, Allie, if you want a good husband," he added solemnly.

I couldn't believe the kid! I did remember Mom telling us how important it was to pray for the person we were going to marry someday, but I hadn't realized how seriously my brother had taken her advice! What a funny kid!

I came to realize later, this "funny kid" brother of mine was rapidly becoming a real prayer warrior! When I finally moved out of the uncomfortable teenage years, and felt pretty confident about myself, Mom shared with me a prayer she had heard John praying a few years earlier.

One night when she went to tuck him in, he seemed to be having a very serious conversation with God about *me*. "And dear Lord, please help my sister Allie. Please make her pretty and give her lots of friends. Thank you. Amen."

That story brought quick tears to my eyes. So he knew what a tough time I had in junior high? He had actually prayed for me? I quickly realized that I had my little brother to thank for the friends I had eventually made and for the fact that my face finally became somewhat pretty, as I grew up.

I have to give the credit for my brother's determination in prayer to my mother. She told us over and over again how important it was to pray, not only for ourselves, but also for our friends and for our family. We prayed together at breakfast every day, and she challenged us as a family to keep track of these prayers in a little notebook. She even bought each of us our own notebooks for our personal prayers. Mom explained to us that God *always* answers our prayers. He doesn't always answer them the way we wish he would, but he *does* reply—usually with "Yes," "No," or "Not right now." As we look back through those little notebooks, we can see years of God's answers to our prayers.

Mom taught us to pray not only by letting us hear her prayers, but by her actions as well. We saw her praying for us again and again. When I was in elementary school and my brothers and sisters were even younger, Mom organized a group of neighborhood women to meet and pray for our schools. Fifteen years later, they are still praying and the results have been truly miraculous! Teachers that we knew were miserable and without hope have come to know and to love God. Administrators who were antagonistic toward Christian students have left, and things are changing in positive ways every day. As children, it gave us great faith in the power of prayer to see our mother so committed to it and to see real results!

My little brother hasn't married yet, so we don't really know how God is going to answer his request for a wife with "smooth hair"! We do know, however, that God heard those earnest prayers of a little boy and that he treasures those prayers. The Bible says that the prayers of God's people are like "golden bowls of incense" (Rv 5:8). Oh, how our heavenly Father loves to hear his children pray!

Thanks, Mom, for teaching us the importance of prayer. You showed us that it doesn't matter how or when we pray but that we can talk to God anytime and anywhere. Thank you for praying for us and with us and for gathering other mothers to pray for our schools. We have seen so much happen as a direct result of your prayers!

Worth the Inconvenience

❦

As a child, my most treasured gift was a small silver cross on a delicate silver chain. I can't explain why it was so special; it just was.

One morning, when I was eight years old, I jumped out of bed to get ready for school. Scrambling to get dressed before breakfast, I suddenly realized that my cross wasn't around my neck. I panicked as I searched frantically for it. I couldn't find it anywhere. I called Mom who was busy getting kids up, fixing breakfast, and making lunches. With three younger children, the last thing she had time for was a weepy child who couldn't find something. But Mom made the time. She sensed that this was very important to me. She stopped what she was doing and came to my room, and together we searched everywhere. We finally found the cross when we took apart all of the bedding. It was wrapped up in a sheet.

Now this may seem like a little thing—just helping a child find a lost item, but Mom's actions communicated to me (although I couldn't have articulated it at that time) that I was important. I was worth Mom's being inconvenienced.

In my late teens, I thought I was really in love. However, Mom and Dad didn't like the boy. They felt he was unmotivated, unreliable, and just plain not "good enough" for their daughter. As a college freshman, I was convinced they were being judgmental and unfair. After an intense freshman year of partying, this love of mine failed his way out of school. I was left with a broken heart and a feeling of humiliation before my parents.

Mom could have said, "I told you so." But following the wise advice of one of her friends, she came to me and said, "Anne, I want you to know that I realize what a crisis this is for you. I've been thinking of this from your perspective and I realize that you are really hurting." Putting her arms around me she continued, "I am so sorry and I want you to know that I ache for your hurt and disappointment." And then she simply held me quietly while I cried.

We both knew that she and Dad had been right in their assessment of this young man. But she didn't mention that. She realized that what I needed most was simply an understanding of my hurt and the reassurance that this hurt was OK.

From the perspective of a whole lifetime these events may seem like small, unimportant issues. But the fact that I still remember them shows me they were significant. I learned from my own mother, and now I'm challenged as a mother of four boys to be sensitive to their needs, even in the seemingly little things. I have learned that it is in the small issues of life that the big lessons are learned.

Thank you, Mom, for taking the time to be sensitive to my needs even when it was inconvenient or when I was wrong. Your sensitivity gave me the assurance that what I thought and felt was important.

My Mother, the Eye

"The Eye." That's what all the kids in the neighborhood called my mother. She seemed to see and know everything we were doing—especially when we were being naughty.

I was one of four kids. My sister Lee and I were in the middle and we were the wild ones. For some reason we always seemed to get caught in our transgressions.

When I was fourteen I snuck out one night with a friend—in my mother's car! Of course I didn't have my license yet, but that didn't stop us. We just *had* to go cruising! We cruised that car right into a large ditch! I was one scared teenager when I had to wake my folks in the middle of the night and explain that the car was miles away in a ditch. Mamma was just thankful for the ditch God had provided to keep us from going any farther!

Then there was the smoking episode. Having grown up with "the Eye" I was careful to hide my cigarettes. When I smoked, I would open my bedroom window to blow the smoke out so she wouldn't smell it. But I forgot about those ashes that piled up on the window sill! One afternoon Mom walked in, and looking at the ashes she said, "So,

Molly, have you been smoking?" Seeing the ashes for the first time, I knew I was caught—again. The "Eye" had seen again.

Mamma not only had eyes, she also had ears, and they were attuned to the Lord. For as long as I can remember, every Wednesday morning "the ladies" showed up at our house for their weekly prayer meeting. Lee and I called them the "Buzzing Bees." We always made sure we escaped before they arrived. We did *not* want to be asked by them if they could pray over us!

They prayed anyway! These moms knew that even though they had special eyes and ears, it was ultimately God who would take care of their children. They claimed his promises:

> My eyes will watch over them for their good, and I will bring them back to this land.... I will give them a heart to know me, that I am the Lord.   JEREMIAH 24:6-7

Once when she was young, my sister Lee and a boy snuck out at night to a field to smoke marijuana. Just as they were rolling their cigarettes, Lee thought she heard someone call her name. Could it be "the Eye" could see her even there in the dark, far from home? She was so terrified that she dropped the marijuana and ran home. Lee knew that though she might have been able to occasionally fool Mamma, with those "Buzzing Bees" praying so constantly it was hard to fool God. His eyes and ears were even better than Mamma's.

All those years Mamma prayed. She often said, "Lord, I don't know where my girls are or what they are doing, but you do." And, of course, he did. At the age of twenty I was tired, lonely, and frustrated. I finally heard God's voice and I gave my life to him.

Now as Lee and I raise our own kids, we, too, have those special "mother's eyes." But we both know that God's eyes are much better than ours and ultimately it's all up to him. His love, his wisdom, and his power are stronger than a mother's. What a relief it is to know that we, too, have him to call on as we raise our kids!

Thank you, Mamma, for having sharp eyes and ears, for not missing much, and for catching us in our transgressions. But thank you most of all for demonstrating to us that real power comes from God. How reassuring and comforting it is to know that he has his eyes on our children!

Never Give Up

I f you met our friend Antley at a party, you would immediately be drawn to his vibrant personality. His enthusiasm for the Lord radiates in his smile and his spirit. Antley's commitment to the Lord is clearly observable in all areas of his life, from his ministry to students in Young Life, to his commitment to his wife, Laura, and his young son, Chase. However, Antley is quick to explain that he has not always been so excited about his relationship with the Lord. He credits his current love for the Lord to his mother and her persistent attempts to draw him to the Lord as a young man.

When Antley was in the ninth grade, he asked Jesus into his life and committed to following him. It was the "commitment" part that gave him problems, though. He was a lot more committed to having a good time with his friends than he was to developing a relationship with the Lord! Even though he considered himself a Christian, Antley really didn't know what that had to do with his day-to-day life. He went to church only at his mother's insistence because he knew it was extremely important to her. Often, it was easier to devise a plan to get out of going to church than it was to get himself into church!

"Some weekends I created the most elaborate lies," Antley remembers. "I would tell Mom I was going to go to the early service. I'd set my alarm for early in the morning. When it went off, I would get out of bed and hide on the floor between the bed and the wall, where I would go back to sleep for a few hours. When Mom would come in to make sure I'd made it out the door to church, she'd see my empty bed and assume I'd gone! She went to the late service, so she didn't know I actually never showed up for the early one! And on the weeks when I had to carry the cross during the service because I was an acolyte (at Mom's insistence, of course!), more often than not I did my duty with a hangover from the night before. I stayed away from the church youth group, too. The group meeting was held on Sunday evenings and that was my time to go surfing and hit the bars with my friends."

In spite of Antley's rebelliousness against being in church on Sundays and his unwillingness to change his rowdy lifestyle, he still had an interest in spiritual things. His mother made every possible effort to encourage him in these activities. "She paid for me to go to Young Life camp five different times!" Antley says. "That's unheard of! I still can't believe she did that for me. I heard about the Lord over and over again, both through Young Life and at church. I don't know why it didn't sink in at that point in my life!"

Throughout all of Antley's high school years, his

mom kept on dragging him to church. "It's not that I hated church," Antley explains, "it's just that I didn't want to be there on Sunday mornings or Sunday evenings! I thought I had better things to do. Thank goodness Mom was praying for me constantly during those years of my life. I know her prayers made a big difference. They kept me from rejecting the faith altogether. I just couldn't seem to get away from the part of me that was drawn to God. I used to sneak into the little prayer chapel at our church late at night during the week and sit there and try to talk to God. I tried to figure out what was wrong with me. Why was I making such a mess of my life? I did everything I wasn't supposed to do—drugs, drinking, sex. You name it, I did it. I think my mom knew alot of what I did, but there wasn't much she could do to stop me. She tried to talk to me, but I wouldn't listen. She even left a copy of the book *Handling Your Hormones* on my bed one time! Of course I didn't read it. I thought I was handling everything just fine! The most amazing thing is that Mom always held on to her hopes for me. She knew the Lord had special plans for me, and she believed in me, even when I didn't believe in myself. She never ever gave up on me, even when I deceived her, embarrassed her, and hurt her over and over again. She prayed, she took me to church even when I didn't want to be there, and she loved me. Even though I did not honor my commitment to Christ, he honored *his* commitment to me, and often he did so through my mom. She was 'Jesus with skin on' to me."

Antley's life began to change when he went away to college. He found friends who challenged him to take his relationship with the Lord seriously and to work at living out his faith. He became involved with Young Life as a volunteer leader and is now a full-time Young Life staff member. He married a girl who is committed to Christ and who, like his mother, fully recognizes Antley's flaws but loves him in spite of them. Looking back at his teen years, Antley is full of gratitude to his mother.

"It's funny. Even though I hated going to church all those years, I'm so glad Mom dragged me there. It amazes me what I learned without meaning to! I have a great understanding of the Old Testament. I know more parables and Bible stories than I can count. I learned so much that is important to me now. I also have a real appreciation for the sacraments and for the functions of the church as a whole that I wouldn't have if Mom hadn't encouraged me to go to church with her for so many years. It's like I just stored it all in my mind somewhere and finally, when I was ready to serve the Lord and only the Lord, I could pull out all that I had heard for so long and make use of it. I'm sure Mom thought that everything was going in one ear and out the other, but it wasn't. Thank the Lord she kept taking me with her. Thank goodness, she never gave up!"

Thanks, Mom, for your perseverance with me. I'm sure there were days when you just wanted to give up on me, days when I hurt you beyond words. Thank you for not giving up hope. Thank you for taking me to church, for telling me that you loved me, and for showing me you believed in me. I am especially thankful that you never stopped praying. You were like the persistent friend in Luke 11— you never gave up. Thank you!

I Was Chosen

I t was time for bed and I really didn't mind too much. It meant Mommy would smooth my sheets and crawl in my bed with me. I'd snuggle in her arms and she'd rub my hair and tell me how special I was and how much she loved me. If it wasn't too late and Mommy wasn't too tired I might get to hear The Story before we said our prayers together.

I never grew tired of hearing her tell The Story. It was so special because it was about me. I was an only child and I was adopted. Mommy would begin by saying, "Your Daddy and I always wanted a baby. We wanted one for so long, and we kept praying that I would get pregnant and have a baby. But after several years when I didn't get pregnant, we began to realize that God had something even better for us. He decided that he was going to give us a very special baby—a baby that another lady was not able to take care of. He wanted parents who would be just right for this very special baby. Guess who that very special baby was! You!"

"Mommy, tell me about the day you got me."

"Well, Tucker," she would continue, "That was the most exciting day in my life! It began when the telephone rang, and a voice on the other end said,

'Mrs. Freeman, your beautiful little baby girl has just been born. Would you like to come see her?'

"I called your daddy at the office and he raced home and got me and we hurried to the hospital. At first we stood outside the window where all the new babies were and just looked at them, trying to figure out which one was you! When we got to the end of the row of babies, there you were and you turned your head and looked at us and seemed to smile!

"We couldn't wait to take you home and introduce you to our family and friends. When we drove up in front of our house, there were lots of friends who had come to see you and to bring you presents! You have always been such a gift to us. Why, the smartest thing Daddy and I ever did in our lives was adopt you!"

Each time Mother told me The Story she got excited. She never tired of telling it, and I never got tired of hearing her tell it. From the beginning she made me feel that being adopted was tremendously special, that I had somehow been chosen.

When I was about seven months pregnant with my own child, my mother came to visit. It was one of those really uncomfortable days, and the baby was kicking non-stop. As I groaned and held my stomach, my mother said, "It must be amazing to feel her kick."

Suddenly, it dawned on me that my mother had never felt a baby inside her womb.

"Mother," I said, "come and put your hands on

my stomach. I want you to feel your grandchild."

The look of awe on my mother's face as she felt her granddaughter kick in the womb was so precious for me. I realized that I was able to give my mother a gift she had not been able to experience personally. She had given me so many gifts and finally I was able to share a very personal one with her.

Thank you, Mother, for helping me know that adopting me is the most special thing that ever happened to you. The security you gave me has helped me to understand how precious it is to be especially chosen by God and to be adopted as his child.

The Mother I Never Had

∽∾

Dot is in heaven. She's home now, Kathy kept reminding herself. In a few minutes it would be her turn to speak in memory of Dot. But at this moment she was overcome with memories, memories of a woman she loved more than any other. What made her feel this way about her mother-in-law?

Dot has always accepted me, Kathy thought to herself with amazed assurance.

My own family was so troubled. My real mother suffered from mental illness and my parents divorced. Although my mother did the best she could, she was not a healthy female role model. It was hard for me to like myself or to feel that anyone else could ever accept me. But from the beginning Dot took me in.

Not long after her son Robert and I became engaged, I had a birthday. Dot planned a big dinner party and invited all the family. She asked me what my favorite foods were and then she prepared them. And she had gifts for me—special ones. She had taken the time to ask what I liked. I wasn't even in her family, yet she made me feel as if I were already an important part of it.

Because I sensed her acceptance, I often turned to her for advice. Oh, she was careful not to offer unsolicited advice or to criticize, but her love for me made me want to ask her for help. Sometimes she merely listened. On other occasions she gave me practical suggestions. She taught me how to cook. She gave me tips on child rearing. Often her best counsel was, "Trust your instincts. You can do this."

Hers was a statement of confidence in me, a confidence I badly needed. Dot demonstrated her love for me again and again by writing me when we lived far away and by ending each phone conversation with, "I love you, Kathy."

She put pictures of us and our kids all over her walls. She was terribly afraid of flying but when we lived overseas, she got on a plane anyway and came to see us. Just knowing how hard that was for her made me appreciate her sacrifice even more.

Kathy sighed. *Oh, how I will miss her.*

Fighting for control, Kathy turned her attention back to the funeral service and realized that it was her turn to speak. Rising from her chair, she slipped past the imposing podium to stand by the casket. She laid her hand on the casket. It made her feel closer to Dot and gave her the confidence to speak what was in her heart:

"In Dot, God gave me the mother I never had. I know she loved me."

Thank you, Dot, for being not only my mother-in-law but, in a real sense, my own mother. Thank you for committing yourself to a frightened and wounded young girl, for accepting me without reservations, and for loving me. From you I have begun to understand God's acceptance, and in his love I have learned to accept myself.

But I Don't Have Anyone!

❧

I t was Mother's Day. A day for celebrating, a day for honoring, and a day when your children overlook your faults and tell you how great you are. A day to honor the mothers in your own life.

It should have been a day of rejoicing. But for Jay and Heather sitting alone in the restaurant, it was a sad reminder of losses. Already in their late forties, they had given up any hope of having children. On this day Heather especially felt the loss that her barrenness represented. Watching a young family at the next table giving their mother gifts didn't help any.

"It just doesn't seem fair," she murmured, while picking at her food. "They are so happy because they have someone."

Her husband Jay tried to cheer her up but he too felt a sense of loss. He had had a difficult year watching his mother die. She had been the last of their parents to go, and now they were all alone with no children of their own to comfort them.

Maybe taking Heather out wasn't such a good idea after all, he thought. *Probably we should have just stayed at home.*

Leaning back in his chair Jay began to glance around the room. His eyes came to rest on a table in the corner. Two elderly women sat quietly eating their salads. One in particular made Jay's heart skip a beat. Wispy white curls framed a slightly pudgy face with a long straight nose. Startled, Jay thought of how much the old woman's profile reminded him of his own mother's. And then he noticed her companion. She too was elderly.

"Heather," he said, "Look at those two women eating alone. They are about the same ages our moms would be if they were alive. I wonder if they have any children?"

Glancing at the women, Heather was silent for a moment.

"They do look awfully alone," she said. "I wonder...."

Suddenly, Heather's face lit up. "Jay," she said, "let's pay for their dinners. But let's not let them know. It can be our Mother's Day gift to them."

Enthusiastic with the change in his wife's mood, Jay called the waitress over and explained that they wanted to pay for the women's dinner in honor of Mother's Day but that it must be anonymous.

Their waitress agreed to help with this special surprise, and Jay and Heather sat back to watch what would happen next. When the women called for their bill, they were told that it was a Mother's Day gift from someone anonymous who wanted to honor them. Shock and pleasure showed in their wrinkled faces as Jay and Heather watched from a few tables away.

But these women were insistent; they had to know.

"Who would do such a kind thing?" they asked.

Finally the poor waitress could no longer keep the secret, and nodding in Jay and Heather's direction she gave the secret away.

Quickly the women made their way over to Jay and Heather's table. Profusely thanking the couple, they asked if they might join them at their table. As introductions were given and stories were shared, a special friendship was begun, one that was to continue throughout the year. This friendship grew and one year later, on Mother's Day, Jay and Heather brought their new "moms" to dinner for a "family" celebration!

Thank you, Lord, that though I don't have a mother or mother-in-law or grandma to honor, you have someone picked out for me. You have in mind some lonely person that needs me, someone that I can care for. Show me who that person is, for you have taught me, "More blessed is he who gives than receives."

Thanks, Mom, for...

_____

_____

_____

_____

_____

_____

_____

_____

_____

_____

Other Books by Allison Yates Gaskins and Susan Alexander Yates

Tightening the Knot: Couple Tested Ideas to Keep Your Marriage Strong, Piñon Publishers, 1995,
ISBN: 0-89109-905-0

Other Books by Susan Alexander Yates

And Then I Had Kids: Encouragement for Mothers of Young Children, Word Publishers, 1988,
ISBN: 08499-3456-7

What Really Matters at Home: Eight Crucial Elements for Building Character in Your Family, co-author, John W. Yates, Word Publishers, 1992,
ISBN: 08499-3416-8

A House Full of Friends: How to Like the Ones You Love, Focus on the Family Publishers, 1995,
ISBN: 1-56179-409-0